Messy Mourning

Hope for Mothers Grieving the Loss of a Child by Suicide

Jackie M. Baker

Published by hope*books
2217 Matthews Township Pkwy
Suite D302
Matthews, NC 28105
www.hopebooks.com

hope*books is a division of hope*media

Printed in the United States of America

First paperback edition.
Paperback ISBN: 979-8-89185-412-3
Hardcover ISBN: 979-8-89185-413-0
Ebook ISBN: 979-8-89185-414-7
Library of Congress Number: 2026938503

Endorsements

For Christian families and friends grieving a death by suicide, Jackie M. Baker has written the essential guide to healing. Sharing poignant personal stories after her own son took his life, Jackie weaves her faith journey along with practical advice and theological wisdom to help others navigate sorrow. If you have ever wondered how to help a friend survive the unimaginable, this book is the gift to give not only to them but to yourself.

—Kathy Izard
Author, *The Hundred Story Home*
and *Trust the Whisper*

In *Messy Mourning,* Jackie M. Baker invites the reader, specifically a Christian mother who has lost a child to suicide, to sit down at her table and listen to her story of loss and the story of the God of the Bible, who understands her because He also has a story of loss. She takes the reader to a place where, through faith, community, and healthy healing processes, they can embrace the pain and still say, "It is Well with My Soul."

—Brad Harper,
Author of *Space at the Table: Conversations between an Evangelical Theologian and His Gay Son* and co-author of *Exploring Ecclesiology: An Evangelical and Ecumenical Introduction*

Trigger Warning

Messy Mourning: Hope for Mothers Grieving the Loss of a Child by Suicide addresses themes of grief, loss, and the profound pain experienced by mothers who have lost a child to suicide. The content includes honest and sometimes graphic depictions of mourning, emotional distress, and personal stories of bereavement.

If you are currently struggling with thoughts of self-harm, suicide, or overwhelming grief, please know you are not alone. Consider reaching out to a mental health professional, church pastor and staff, other trusted support networks, or a crisis hotline for help. Your feelings are valid, and support is available.

Readers who may be sensitive to these topics are encouraged to take care of themselves and exercise discretion before proceeding. This book is intended as a source of hope and understanding, but the journey through its pages can be emotionally intense. Please read at your own pace and take breaks as needed.

Author's Note

The events and stories presented in this book are based on fact. Details have been reconstructed to the best of my recollection, drawing on my journals, essays, and e-mails. Specific names and locations have been changed to protect confidentiality. Additionally, in several chapters, the chronology may have been condensed or altered to enhance narrative flow and account for variations in memory associated with the grieving process following Sebastian's loss.

In Chapter 7, the term "church" (with a lowercase "c") is used to refer to the church as a whole rather than to an individual congregation, unless otherwise specified. This chapter does not include a discussion of "assisted suicide" or "death with dignity" legislation.

This book is dedicated to

every mother who has lost a child by suicide.

"He reached down from on high and took hold of me;
he drew me out of deep waters.
He rescued me from my powerful enemy,
from my foes, who were too strong for me.
They confronted me in the day of my disaster,
but the Lord was my support.
He brought me out into a spacious place;
he rescued me because ***he delighted in me.****"*
Psalm 18:16–19 (emphasis added)

"Blessed are those who mourn, for they will be comforted."
Matthew 5:4

Cemetery

Flat gravestones perfectly lined up in neat, clean rows.
Permanent reminders of those now gone, never to return.
Tranquil yet tragic memorials are displayed for all to see.
Lone mourners, crying, weeping, longing, wondering why.
Peace and tranquility can be found here,
favoring those who yearn for it.
Soon forgotten pilgrimages, thwarted by current
life woes.

—Jackie M. Baker

Acknowledgements

There have been thousands of words written over the last eight years as I struggled with the loss of Sebastian. It would have been impossible to complete this book without the unwavering support of family and friends who surrounded Steve, Isabel, and me, offering encouragement, prayers, and invaluable assistance. The hundreds of meals, cards, gifts, prayers, and time extended to our family throughout the days, months, and years following Sebastian's death have been instrumental in our healing journey.

Our family is exceedingly fortunate to be a part of New Heights Church. I can't say enough about how our church family walked alongside us, doing extraordinary things for us (most of which I still don't remember), but Steve remembers and reminds me when I ask. When Steve notified our church, many people dropped what they were doing and came to us immediately. We would never have made it through without them, and I am deeply grateful to every one of them.

Eight years ago, I enrolled in an online memoir class to facilitate my writing process and reflect on my grief journey after the loss of my son. After completing thirteen sessions, I joined a writers' cohort comprising five accomplished professional women, all of whom were engaged in writing memoirs and essays. We called ourselves the Memoir Mavens and began our initial meeting, conducted via ZOOM, during the COVID-19 pandemic. We convened regularly for five years, during which I significantly developed my writing skills. The members of this group, the Memoir Mavens, provided invaluable encouragement, constructive feedback, and guidance that enabled me to cultivate my unique voice and refine my craft. With their support, I explored writing techniques such as "showing" instead of "telling" and discovered my love for braided essays. Their early input was instrumental in the beginning of this book. Thank you, Catherine, Sharon, Eve, Martha, and Rosemarie, for your profound impact on my writing journey.

I would like to especially acknowledge the following individuals for their support during the writing of this book:

Jaron & Teresa, my prayer warriors. Thank you both for walking with me in my grief journey. You lived this book with me. You both listened and prayed for me as I cried for what seemed like years at our bimonthly prayer meetings. Thank you for letting me shed many tears in your homes. I love you both.

Cheryl, my fellow sister in grief and beta reader. We have cried many tears over these last seven years; many tears. But now we can laugh more because we know we couldn't do this without Jesus. I look forward to the day when we see Sebastian, Tom, and Graeme again.

Brad & Robin, you loved Sebastian as a son and wept with us in our loss. You met with us, loved us, cared for us, and let us talk. You were our advocates and sane voices of reality as we struggled with what happened to us. You helped Steve and me wade through our theological and heart issues, and we love you both. Your friendship is important to us. Brad, I appreciate your time and expertise in reviewing my manuscript and for ensuring the accuracy of its theological content.

Matt & Cindy, you both have been my spiritual parents since the day I met you. Thank you for believing in me when I was a struggling young woman many years ago. Thank you for "giving me away" at my marriage to Steve and for dedicating Sebastian as an infant (I still remember how Matt held up Sebastian for the entire congregation to see his baptismal outfit at his baby dedication). And thank you, Matt, for speaking the truth about Jesus at Sebastian's memorial service.

Kathy, for believing in me and encouraging me to write this book. You saw the vision and need even when others didn't. I'll never forget your words, "You have to write this book." Thank you for editing my early drafts. Your comments were spot-on and helpful. I'm incredibly thankful I picked you as my writing coach. You are more than a coach; we've become friends.

Grant & Amy, for all Starbucks drinks and dinners. Your friendship has been invaluable throughout these past years. Thanks, Grant, for letting me cry while you cut my hair over the last eight years.

J.P., for loving Sebastian and caring for him no matter where he was.

Betsy & Kevin, we bonded before we "betrothed our firstborns" in our wombs. Thank you, Kevin, for letting Betsy come and take Sebastian's belongings when I couldn't look in his room. Thank you, Betsy, for always encouraging my writing and being a beta reader. Your comments and suggestions are always invaluable.

Joelle, for editing my first manuscripts. You taught me how to write stories.

Diane, for helping Steve function and praying for us. You are such a prayer warrior.

Teresa V, my headshots and web design are beautiful. You are truly gifted.

Steve, you are my rock and my world. You always bring me back to Jesus. Thank you for allowing me to mourn in my messy ways these eight years. Who knew that Sebastian's loss would bring us even closer as a couple and even closer to Jesus? How we loved Sebastian, our firstborn son. He kept us on our knees. We would not be able to share Sebastian's story without first telling Jesus' story. Thank you for allowing me to share Sebastian's life; for this reason, others might come to know Jesus better.

Isabel, my sweet girl, you have always been my biggest supporter. I don't have words that can fully capture how much I love you, but I know you feel it. Thank you for letting me share your stories about Sebastian; remembering him together has brought us comfort and kept his memory alive in our hearts. I'll always cherish the nights we sat together, looking through old photos and sharing laughter and tears over our favorite Sebastian moments. You loved your brother deeply, and I know you miss him. Thank you for letting us get matching Sebastian tattoos—a beautiful reminder that he's always with us, woven into our lives and love.

Brennan, I appreciate the care and support you have shown Isabel. From the day of Sebastian's passing, you became a member of our family. Although you never met Sebastian, your presence during that challenging time was invaluable. Thank you for your patience and understanding as we navigated through our messy mourning. Your character was evident throughout the difficulties we faced, and I remember your willingness to assist and comfort us, even when my memories were unclear. I am grateful to have you as my son-in-law.

Hope*books, for supporting and encouraging me in my publishing journey.

Jesus, my Lord & Savior. My book says it all.

Table of Contents

Foreward

In the middle of the night on September 19, 2017, my wife, Robin, was sleeping next to me when she received a text from our dear friend, Jackie M. Baker. Her son, Sebastian, was dead, and he had taken his own life. We were in shock. Sebastian had spent a great deal of time with us in our home, as he and our youngest were very close. However, it was not the first time I had received such a text, phone call, or sat across my desk from someone whose child had died. During my thirteen-year tenure as a pastor, these tragic notifications happened way too often. Parents are not supposed to outlive their children; it's simply not the way it is supposed to be. Unfortunately, most of us know someone, whether it is at work, at church, or on the sidelines of our kids' soccer games, who has lost a child. Some have lost babies or young children to disease; some have lost adolescent children to a car accident. Perhaps those parents to whom we know least what to say are those whose children have died by suicide. For these parents, there is a whole array of issues that go beyond crippling grief to questions about guilt, failure, and constant second-guessing about what they could have done differently to prevent this heartbreaking tragedy.

The book you hold in your hand is not just the story of Jackie M. Baker's journey to survive, process, and even grow from the grief of losing her son. It is also a guidebook for those walking the same road. Furthermore, it serves as a valuable resource for friends and family who want to support their loved ones during times of suffering. For those mourning the loss of a child, Jackie speaks a language that only they understand because she lives in their world. For those wanting to help, Jackie illustrates the kinds of actions and words that actually bring help and comfort versus those well-meaning ones that often increase pain and exacerbate anxiety. This is also a book for people of faith who seek to understand how the purposes of a loving God can connect to the grief and confusion that accompany loss due to suicide.

After finishing Jackie's book and taking some time to consider what most impacted me, several things came to mind.

Throughout this book, Jackie's seminary degree in Biblical Studies and Theology profoundly affects the way she handles complex issues and serves as a helpful resource for her illustrations. She uses stories from the Bible to help readers cope with loss and grief. She takes us to the incarnation of God in Jesus Christ, drawing us to recognize that God knows what it is like to lose a son. In short, for those who walk this road of suffering, God understands them, not just intellectually, but also experientially.

One of the most powerful writing techniques Jackie employs is the inclusion of journal entries as she processed the loss of Sebastian. In these, she takes us from description to experience, inviting the reader to join her as she cries out to God and works through the stages of grief.

Losing her son also led Jackie to address the question all grieving parents ask: “Is there something I could have done differently to prevent this from happening?” Here, Jackie confronts the myth that we can control our adult children, which provides her with a foundation for recognizing that, as believers, we have to trust our kids to God, knowing that this does not ensure they will turn out okay, but that whatever happens, God is good. As she walks us through this issue, Jackie’s theological acumen comes into play as she addresses the age-old struggle with evil. Specifically, in her case, “Can I really believe that God is loving and in control of all things if he allows my beloved child to take his life?” It is a fair question, and one that the church often answers simplistically. Jackie takes us beyond simple solutions to a place of accepting the tension that even in a broken world where heartbreaking and destructive things happen every day, God is indeed still good and can be trusted.

Another essential element of Jackie’s book is that she counsels grieving parents to move beyond themselves and into the church. She understands that a necessary aspect of healing is community, specifically support groups and the church. Support groups provide the kind of help that can only come from those who have “been there.” And in the church, fellow believers can, in truth, support the healing presence of Christ.

Jackie muses on how the Biblical idea of the future can be drawn back into the present to offer hope to grieving parents. The Christian conviction that this life is not all there is does not mean that Christian funerals should be happy, but it tempers our grief with the assurance that relationships are not forever ended by death.

One last aspect of Jackie's book that will be helpful to readers is the set of questions at the end of each chapter, which encourages the reader to draw the principles and ideas from the book into their personal story. This technique transforms the text from being simply a record of Jackie's journey into a purposeful means for the reader's own growth and development.

In *Messy Mourning,* Jackie's invites the reader, specifically a Christian mother who has lost a child to suicide, to sit down at her table and listen to her story of loss and the story of the God of the Bible, who understands her because He also has a story of loss. She takes the reader to a place where, through faith, community, and healthy healing processes, they can embrace the pain and still say, "It is Well with My Soul."

—Brad Harper,
Author of *Space at the Table* and
co-author of *Exploring Ecclesiology*
Retired Professor of Theology,
Multnomah University and Biblical Seminary

SECTION ONE

The Unexpected Storm

"As for everyone who comes to me and hears my words and puts them into practice, I will show you what they are like. They are like a man building a house, who dug down deep and laid the foundation on rock. When a flood came, the torrent struck that house but could not shake it, because it was well built. But the one who hears my words and does not put them into practice is like a man who built a house on the ground without a foundation. The moment the torrent struck that house, it collapsed, and its destruction was complete."

—Luke 6:47–49

CHAPTER 1

The Club No Mother Wanted to Join

"The crime of suicide lies rather in its disregard for the feelings of those whom we leave behind."[1]
—E.M. Forster

Journal Entry—June 19, 2019:

"Mom! Mom! Wake up! The police are here!"

I knew in that moment that Sebastian was dead.

Six Septembers ago, my daughter woke me up screaming.

Six Septembers ago, my son ended his life by suicide. I remember my daughter Isabel, Sebastian's sister, screaming

1 Forster, E. M. *Howards End.* Penguin Books, 2000.

for me to wake up. The police were at the door. It was after midnight. Police only come to the door at that time if something awful has happened. And it had.

Six Septembers ago, I have little memory of what was said or what had happened in the ensuing days and weeks.

I do remember the police chaplain saying Sebastian had been in an accident and had fallen off Smith Rock, a state park located in the high desert of Central Oregon, near Bend. He had been kicked out of a rehab facility the day before and was staying in a homeless shelter. I had talked to Sebastian a couple of hours before. I didn't know his last words to me, "I love you, Mom," would be the last words I would ever hear from my son's lips. We had made plans to see him that weekend. He was going to meet his sister's boyfriend for the first time.

When the police said he had fallen, I somehow replied calmly, "He didn't fall".

"Are you sure?"

"Yes, it was intentional." He fell, but it was no accident.

Six months earlier, Sebastian had tried to hang himself, but the rope had broken. I can still see the rope burns around his neck; their red and purple bruises are permanently seared in my memory bank.

"I'm sorry, Mom. I couldn't help myself."

We tried to help our son. For over five years, we struggled to get him help, but finally, on September 19, 2017, he chose to end his own suffering.

But our suffering was only beginning.

Six Septembers ago, I joined an ever-growing group of mothers who had lost a child to suicide.

My mother, at the young age of thirty-six, died suddenly when I was only eighteen. At her graveside service, my grandmother leaned over to me, clenched my hand, and said, "No mother should ever have to bury her children." She looked me in the eye, tears flowing nonstop, "I should have died first."

Fifty-five years later, I knew how she felt.

All people will experience grief and mourning, but I believe losing a child to suicide is different. Most people don't know what to say after your child takes their own life, but when a child dies of cancer, everybody rejoices in how brave the child was and says that they were a hero. Friends, family, and strangers are amazed by the family's steadfast perseverance as they advocate and care for their dying child. As their child takes a final breath, the family surrounds the bedside, keeping a constant vigil until the end. The family has a sense of closure as they kiss their child, tell them that Mom and Dad will always love them, and give them one final goodbye.

If a child dies in an accident, people usually feel sad about this young person's untimely death. Such a tragedy; a life cut short when their life was just beginning.

When someone dies by suicide, no one says they fought their mental health issue bravely, only for the disease to take their life. Friends and acquaintances might say how tragic it was that your child died, and they are sorry for your loss. People often struggle to find the right words or ways to support those affected by the decisions made by another's child. I have learned over these last years that many people are afraid that they might say the wrong thing, especially if they are Christians. Church history has not always been kind to those who have died by suicide. Even though there have been steps taken to help alleviate the shame and guilt associated with suicide, the stigma remains. In my early grief, I felt the unspoken stigma of being a Christian parent who lost their child, who had also professed their faith in Jesus, to suicide. According to people in certain denominations of the protestant church, Sebastian was selfish for taking his own life.[2] He had sinned because he had broken the fifth commandment: "You shall not murder" (Exodus 20:13). *Could Sebastian even be forgiven if he was already dead?* I frequently heard well-meaning people comment, "Oh, he's with Jesus now." *Did they really mean that phrase, or were they just saying something to say something?*

In 1983, the Catholic Church formally acknowledged that suicide was not a mortal sin. According to the *Catechism of the Catholic Church*: "For a sin to be mortal, three conditions must together be met: 'Mortal sin is sin whose object is grave matter, and which is also committed with full knowledge and deliberate consent.'"[3] At the same time, the Catholic Church still asserts that "suicide contradicts the natural inclination of the human being to preserve and perpetuate his life. Suicide is contrary to love for the

2 Bierly, Steve R. *A Christian View of Suicide*. CreateSpace Independent Publishing Platform, 2017.

3 IV. The Gravity of Sin: Mortal and Venial Sin." Catechism of the Catholic Church, Vatican, www.vatican.va/content/catechism/en/part_three/section_one/chapter_one/article_8/iv_the_gravity_of_sin_mortal_and_venial_sin.html.

living God."[4] The Catholic Church has made concessions in the case of "grave psychological disturbances, anguish, or grave fear of hardship, suffering, or torture (that) can diminish the responsibility of the one committing suicide."[4] Despite these exceptions, the ongoing unspoken stigma surrounding suicide still exists within churches, primarily due to inadequate education and biblical understanding. (See Chapter 8 for a more in-depth discussion on this topic.)

This book is a guide for grieving mothers who have lost a child to suicide and for those who want to support them. It is specifically designed for mothers with a Christian faith background, offering practical advice and spiritual comfort to help them navigate the challenging journey of grief. The book aims to show that, despite the pain and messiness of mourning, there is still beauty amidst the brokenness.

Messy Mourning also serves as a resource for those who know a grieving mother and want to help support her in her messy mourning. There are many books on grief and suffering (see Appendix). I'm not trying to write that book, but there are not many books written by a Christian mother who has lost a child to suicide. It's been eight years since my son Sebastian took his life. Since that time, I have made an effort to understand the events that transpired. As the days transitioned into weeks and the weeks into years, and now, as I approach the next decade since my son's passing, my sole source of strength and resilience has been my unwavering faith in Jesus. This faith has been my anchor, comfort, and hope in the darkest times.

---

4 "I. Respect for Human Life." Catechism of the Catholic Church, Vatican, www.vatican.va/archive/ENG0015/__P7Z.HTM.

I'm a different person; one changed forever by this tragedy, but also one who has learned that God still loves me. God undeniably loved me so much that he sent His Son to die for me that I might be set free from the guilt, shame, and doubts that assailed me before and after my son's death. God watched His Son die. He watched my son die. He knows my pain. I want others who have lost a child to suicide to know that God loves them in their pain and God is with them even in those darkest nights when all hope seems lost. God was with me in those worst moments when I couldn't breathe, sleep, or eat, and all I did was cry. God brought me out of this deep, dark place because he delighted in me and loved me in my pain (Psalm 18:19, 2 Samuel 22:20).

Research studies have shown that individuals who have lost a child to suicide, including mothers, often experience grief differently compared to those who have lost a child by other causes.[5] Everyone who loses someone tends to follow a five-step grieving process that Dr. Elizabeth Kubler Ross first recognized and wrote about in the 1960s. These initial five stages of grief included denial, anger, bargaining, depression, and acceptance.[6] In addition to these five stages, mothers grieving the loss of a child to suicide, the journey through messy mourning

---

5 Lynn, Cynthia Walker. *"The Lived Experience of Mothers Bereaved by the Suicide Death of a Child."* 2011. *Electronic Theses and Dissertations*, paper 1285, East Tennessee State University, https://dc.etsu.edu/etd/1285.

6 Kübler-Ross, Elisabeth, and David Kessler. On Grief & Grieving: Finding the Meaning of Grief through the Five Stages of Loss. Simon & Schuster, 2005.

can be especially complex. After the shock begins to wear off, many mothers experience persistent ruminations about the circumstances and consequences of the death, along with overwhelming feelings of guilt, shame, and self-blame.[7] Unlike other forms of bereavement, suicide loss often brings relentless questions about "why" and "what could have been done," which can intensify isolation and self-doubt. C. S. Lewis, reflecting on the grief he felt after his wife's death from cancer, poignantly described loss as "an amputation."[8] While Lewis's words speak to the deep pain of grief of losing a spouse, for those impacted by suicide, this sense of irrevocable loss is compounded by a unique and complicated emotional burden.

Compounding a mother's loss is the fact that other family members—such as a spouse, father, and siblings are also experiencing grief. Each person will process their loss in distinct ways (see Chapter 6). For instance, a spouse may struggle with feelings of isolation, while siblings might express their grief through anger or withdrawal. Recognizing these differences is essential for families to support one another more effectively and to foster empathy during such a difficult time.

Sometimes, it's hard to remember that everyone is suffering. That's why mourning is extremely messy. It's easier to turn inward and forget that others are grieving alongside you. A friend of mine, who had also lost a son

7 "Complicated Grief." *Association for Behavioral and Cognitive Therapies*. https://www.abct.org/wp-content/uploads/2021/03/complicated-grief.pdf.

8 Lewis, C. S. *A Grief Observed.* HarperOne, 2015.

to suicide, called to tell me her husband had wanted to make their son's bedroom into an office. It had been a year, and even though my friend's husband was ready "to move forward", she wasn't prepared to make, in her opinion, such a drastic change. She had kept her son's room the same since his death. Her husband may have wanted to move on, but she wasn't ready.

Mourning is a messy process, and individuals do not recover at the same pace. It is essential to be patient with those grieving in a way that differs from what we think is appropriate, while simultaneously providing them with hope that their situation will improve. Even though the present may seem overwhelmingly dark and the light of day difficult to perceive, we must continue to offer support and encouragement.

"Brothers and sisters, we do not want you to be uninformed about those who sleep in death, so that you do not grieve like the rest of mankind, who have no hope. For we believe that Jesus died and rose again, and so we believe that God will bring with Jesus those who have fallen asleep in him...Therefore, encourage one another with these words" (1 Thessalonians 4:13–14,18).

Grief often feels like a battle. It is a relentless, exhausting fight that leaves us searching for the strength to carry on. When the weight of mourning becomes unbearable, it's easy to feel isolated and overwhelmed. Yet, the Bible reminds us that we are never alone in our darkest moments. There's power in community, shared burdens, and finding hope even in the midst of profound heartbreak.

The Bible recounts the story of Moses, who led his people out of slavery in Egypt. God assured them that they would become a mighty nation if they obeyed His commands. This obedience required them to engage in battles with other nations over territory. Moses and the people of Israel had a conflict with the Amalekites. Moses's commander, Joshua, and his army were successful in the battle when Moses, standing on a nearby hill, raised his hands in prayer. However, the Israelites began to lose when Moses lowered his hands due to fatigue. Similarly, as we tire of trying to grieve on our own, Moses couldn't win this battle alone. He needed help from his family and friends. Realizing he needed assistance, Moses received help from his brother Aaron and friend Hur. They provided something for Moses to sit on and supported his hands to keep them steady. With Aaron and Hur's assistance, Moses's hands remained raised, and Joshua's army ultimately won the battle (Exodus 17: 8–13).

Grief is a journey that mothers mourning the loss of a child by suicide should never undertake alone. It necessitates the support of others to assist when one is overwhelmed. During these challenging times, relying on those who have either experienced similar trials or are currently walking alongside this path is vital. This time of mourning is not the moment to avoid troubling others or insist on self-sufficiency by thinking, "I'll be fine." In reality, you may not be fine for an extended period, as complicated grief after losing a child to suicide can be excruciating.

I wrote *Messy Mourning* to support and provide a how-to manual for those who have lost a child to suicide. This book is a guide for mothers who feel misunderstood, isolated, and angry at God and others. It provides resources and strategies for finding help and directs mothers to the same hope that sustained me in my grief. I believe that grieving mothers can find true hope through a relationship with Jesus, who has accompanied me through my darkest nights, even when His presence was not immediately felt. Jesus has remained steadfast throughout my messy mourning, guiding me until I saw beauty once again. Ultimately, much like a house that remains standing after surviving a violent storm, despite the damage (there is always damage), we too can find hope and thrive once again, despite feeling battered and bruised.

We can find peace and beauty in our brokenness again, even amid our messy mourning.

Thank you for letting me accompany you on your grief journey.

THOUGHTS TO CONSIDER

1. Grab a notebook and start writing the first thoughts that come to your mind about "this club" you never wanted to join. There are no wrong answers. Getting your jumbled thoughts down on paper can help you gain clarity as you process your grief.
2. Where does your "help" come from?
3. In what ways have you been trying to cope with what has happened to you? Has it been helpful? Why or why not?
4. What have people said that made you cringe?
5. What have people said that has been helpful?

CHAPTER 2

Finding Hope in Messy Mourning

"Two are better than one, because they have a good return for their labor: If either of them falls down, one can help the other up."
Ecclesiastes 4:9–10

"Praise be to the God and Father of our Lord Jesus Christ, the Father of compassion and the God of all comfort, who comforts us in all our troubles, so that we can comfort those in any trouble with the comfort we ourselves receive from God."
2 Corinthians 1:3–4

I sat near the espresso maker in a church lobby near Bend, Oregon. I tried not to listen to the hissing and gurgling noises as it produced steam, similar to a locomotive working hard to climb a hill. After preparing each coffee, the unusually perky barista repeatedly banged a portafilter in the sink. Streams of people walked in front of me, behind me, and next to me; they were laughing, sharing jokes, hugging, and discussing lunch plans that involved their family and friends. No one seemed to notice me sitting alone on this tall stool, waiting for someone to initiate a conversation.

Our son, Sebastian, had recommended this church; he had attended it a few times during his stay at a nearby inpatient rehabilitation center, and he really liked it. Our family had been driving the three-and-a-half-hour journey from Vancouver, Washington, to Bend, Oregon at least twice a month to support Sebastian in his recovery.

However, Sebastian was not improving as we had hoped. His struggle with mental health issues was taking a toll on him, and consequently, on our family.

Sebastian, who had turned twenty-three in April, had recently been readmitted to a psychiatric unit for two weeks due to worsening suicidal thoughts. He had attempted suicide six months earlier. Sebastian had started on a new medication, Lithium, intended to stabilize and manage the unrelenting voices in his head, but its effectiveness still appeared uncertain. Visiting hours at the hospital began around noon; therefore, my husband Steve and I decided to visit the church Sebastian had recommended before seeing him.

As I sat in the church service, I couldn't help but feel a wave of mixed emotions. The familiar worship songs comforted me, and I found myself raising my hands, tears streaming down my face. I was a part of the congregation, yet I felt significantly alone in my grief, surrounded by people who seemed to have no understanding of the pain I was going through.

After the time of worship ended, a bespeckled, older man, the senior pastor, who appeared to be about my age, came up and began to speak. I don't recall much about the sermon. Still, I do remember him telling the congregation about his one and only son, who had died in a car accident the year before. His son had turned twenty-one.

The pastor, recalling his son's death, got my attention, and I grabbed my husband's hand. Steve gave me a brief smile and turned his head back to the front of the stage. Even though my son was alive, I felt an instant connection with this still-hurting man as he talked about his past year and his intense time of grief and mourning. This father poured out his heart, sharing his struggles and his son's. It was as if God was preparing our hearts for what might happen to us. I sat and pondered the pastor's words in my heart. In a similar way, Jesus' mother had pondered in amazement at the shepherd's word about her son that first Christmas morning. His empathy made me feel less alone in my own grief.

My heart always seemed heavy with pain and sorrow for my boy.

After the service, the pastor invited individuals seeking prayer to proceed to the "wall of prayer" on the left side of the sanctuary. This large, dark wall highlighted the men and women positioned in front of it, prepared to lay hands on and pray for those who asked and needed prayer, comfort, and encouragement.

Steve said, "I'm going to the wall for prayer. I need all the prayer I can get."

I couldn't go with him; I could not do it. Prayer was still a struggle for me. I was angry and confused about why God would allow my son to suffer like this, and I wasn't ready to have some unknown person lay hands on me and pray over me.

I said, "I'll meet you in the lobby."

I left the aisle feeling more alone, caught in the crowd streaming out of the sanctuary, like some salmon fighting upstream, where I eventually ended up by the effervescent coffee-makers.

As I waited for Steve to finish his prayers, I grew increasingly anxious and felt a strong urge to leave the church. As I tried to pray from my seat, I found myself distracted and frustrated by the seemingly cheerful individuals who continued to pass me by, get coffee, and laugh as if they had no cares in the world. My mind wandered to why these people were not more aware of my visible distress. Couldn't they see my pain? At my home church, we are encouraged as a congregation to seek out the stranger and help those who might be in need, yet in this space, I remained invisible. Glancing around for Steve and the nearest exit, I decided to wait outside. Steve could text me for my whereabouts.

“Hello, I saw you sitting here. Is this your first time at our church?” Surprised, I looked up from my phone and saw this woman about my age smiling at me and extending her right hand in greeting. I took it with my sweaty palm and smiled nervously back.

“Yes, my husband and I are visiting. Our son has come here a few times, and he recommended it.”

“Does your son live in Bend?” She seemed genuinely concerned, as if she sincerely cared about me and my thoughts.

Without warning, I blurted everything out in one breath, “For the last four months, my son has been at a rehabilitation program for teens and adults struggling with addictions, but now he’s at the hospital in the psych unit for suicidal thoughts. He’s a mess, but he’s my mess; we’re here to support him and help him where we can.”

She smiled again and told me her name was Meg. “My husband is the senior pastor here.” It suddenly hit me who Meg really was. This was no accidental meeting. God had sent her to me in my distress.

“You lost your son,” I blurted out again, embarrassed by my bluntness. “I’m sorry.”

“It’s been a little over a year,” she said, her voice steady. “His name was Ben. We loved him, and I miss him every day. He had his struggles, too, but I’m comforted by knowing he’s home now. I don’t have to worry about him anymore.” Her words, filled with a quiet strength and acceptance, brought a sense of reassurance and hope to my heart. Despite her own loss, she was able to find comfort, and I found hope in her story.

Her words encouraged me. My son was still alive, but her son was dead, and yet she still reached out to me in my distress. Despite her sufferings, she approached me, probably going out of her comfort zone, and found me among all these people.

She saw the stranger and welcomed me. I was humbled.

We continued to talk, sharing stories about our sons and husbands. We found common ground in our shared experiences, and both tears and laughter marked our conversation. Despite the weight of our grief, we discovered moments of joy and lightness in our shared messiness. Then, she asked if she could pray for me, and I readily accepted. After our Amen, Steve finally arrived, and I introduced him to my new friend. We hugged, said our goodbyes, and I left the church with a renewed sense of hope and connection, knowing we'd soon be back again.

But that sense of hope and connection soon vanished because two weeks later, Sebastian died after falling off Smith Rock.

I've never been back to Bend.

Within days after Sebastian's death, I remembered Meg's kind words that day at her church. Our meeting was no accident. Sebastian, too, was now home in heaven. I, too, didn't have to worry about him anymore. Her words of encouragement were such a comfort to me during the aftermath of Sebastian's suicide. They gave me a glimmer of hope as I struggled to get through each day.

Somehow, I had to let her know.

I didn't recall her last name, but I remembered the name of her church and soon found it online. After browsing the church's website, I discovered her email address. I sent her a quick note, unsure if she would remember me or if my message would end up in her spam folder.

I wrote in the subject box, "My son Sebastian," and the following correspondence began:

9/29/2017

Dear Meg,

You met me at church in between services a couple of weeks ago. I sincerely believe that God directed you to me in your church lobby. Your prophetic words have encouraged me this week. You told me about your son dying a year ago and said he was now home. My son was in the hospital for suicidal thoughts in Bend. You were such an encouragement to me that day. No one else talked to me that busy day between services, but, as I mentioned previously, I know God directed you to me!

My son died Tuesday night, falling off Smith Rock. He's home in heaven now!

Thank you! God is good!

Your sister in Christ, Jackie

Four hours later, I received this reply from her:

Hi Jackie,

I am very sorry for your loss. Every day, I try to balance my loss—that I don't get to see my son again until heaven—with his gain. He's in heaven, enjoying a new and beautiful life with Jesus. My heart goes out to you and your husband, but I also agree with you that Sebastian is home. More alive than ever, in heaven.

I do think we were supposed to meet, as I literally circled back around to greet you. God is good at giving us things to hold onto, even amidst huge, ridiculous waves, and I'm glad our meeting gets to be one of those handholds.

Much Love,

Meg

My reply:

Thank you, Meg; I feel God's presence through the prayers of His people. It's been three weeks now since Sebastian died. Our church held a service in his honor, and over 600 people attended. I had a glimpse of heaven that day. The congregation glorified God at Sebastian's memorial. I am finding daily beauty in my brokenness.

Thank you for your prayers,

Jackie

It had been a little over a year since Sebastian died by suicide when I opened the email document that read, "Can you see Cheryl? She wants to meet with you." Cheryl's husband and son had died two weeks earlier in a tragic diving accident while the family was spending Christmas in Mexico. My stomach began to spasm as I reread our mutual friend's inquiry. I tried to swallow the bile that had risen unexpectedly in my throat.

I can't meet Cheryl.

How can I help her?

Isn't it too soon for me to help?

What would I say?.

I didn't lose my husband, just my son.

Well-meaning friends had been telling me that I should be feeling better. After all, it had been over 365 days since I lost my Sebastian. What most people didn't know is that I still cried almost every day. It felt like my grief was getting worse instead of better in the second year. Was there something wrong with me? Shouldn't I be better? I was moving forward, albeit slowly. Still, then, as I made myself read the Psalms every day, I would reread this familiar lament of King David that I had highlighted in yellow:

> How long, Lord? Will you forget me forever?
> How long will you hide your face from me?
> How long must I wrestle with my thoughts
> and day after day have sorrow in my heart?
> How long will my enemy triumph over me?
> Look on me and answer, Lord my God.
> Give light to my eyes, or I will sleep in death,
> and my enemy will say, 'I have overcome him,'
> and my foes will rejoice when I fall.
> But I trust in your unfailing love;
> my heart rejoices in your salvation.
> I will sing the Lord's praise,
> for he has been good to me (Psalm 13:1–6).

I knew deep down that God wanted me to share my story. As I continued to walk through my grief, I began to recognize how God was working not only in my own life but also in the lives of others around me. It wasn't because I had mastered the art of grieving; comparatively, it was the simple act of sharing the reality of my messy mourning that opened the door for God to move.

When I received that email from my friend, asking if I could meet with Cheryl, the words felt heavy. I remember staring at the screen and reading the message over and over. I wondered if I was ready, if I had anything to offer. But in that moment, I sensed God asking me to step forward and be present.

Looking back, I think about the moment when Meg approached me at that church in Bend. At the perfect time, she reached out and spoke God's hope into my life. Her words were gentle and reassuring. She told me I wasn't alone, and she offered practical comfort when my pain felt overwhelming.

Now, I sense that God is placing me into other people's lives so that I can help them find hope through Him. In the same way, as Meg was there for me, I want to offer compassion and encouragement to those who are hurting, guiding them toward the hope that comes from a relationship with God.

Therefore, with my grieving, heavy heart, I met with Cheryl. I held her hand and cried buckets of tears with her, acknowledging her profound pain like no one else could. Over the past eight years, Cheryl and I have continued to meet, and I have come to comprehend the complexities of this kind of mourning.

Mourning is messy.

Even though mourning is messy and challenging, sharing the burden of grief with others who are also experiencing similar loss can be helpful and life-changing, even though tears of grief are still fresh from our own recent losses. We who have already walked this exhausting and difficult journey can offer solace and help to those currently hurting, guiding them towards the hope that resides in us, which can only come from God. "Let us hold unswervingly to the hope we profess, for he who promised is faithful" (Hebrews 10:23).

If you are reading this and find yourself, or someone you care about, in the midst of messy mourning, please know that you are not alone. My heart is with you, and I want to walk alongside you in your grief, sharing in the honest struggles and tears that come with such a loss, especially after the suicide of someone you love. Whether you find comfort in faith, community, or personal reflection, I hope that these pages offer you support and encouragement in your journey through grief. Throughout these chapters, I will share my own experiences, practical tools for coping, and words of encouragement to help you navigate each step of your healing process. Together, we can find hope even in the darkest places, and as I have found, this hope comes through trusting in Jesus, who understands our pain and suffering.

THOUGHTS TO CONSIDER

1. How can reaching out to others during difficult times help us feel less alone in our grief?
2. What are some ways we might support someone who is struggling with loss, even if we don't have all the answers?
3. How do personal stories of hope and comfort encourage us as we go through our own challenges?
4. Why is it important to recognize that mourning can be complicated and different for everyone?
5. In what ways can faith, community, or personal connections bring hope during times of sorrow?

CHAPTER 3

Sympathy for the Mother of Judas

"So Judas threw the money into the temple and left. Then he went away and hanged himself."
—Matthew 27:5

I know precisely how Judas' mother felt when she heard her son had died by suicide. September 19, 2017, is seared into my memory vault forever.

"No!" she must have cried out. "It can't be true. It has to be a mistake." She probably grabbed her husband by the tunic as he stood next to her. He, too, had heard the words and began to tremble, shaking his head in disbelief. The shock of the news was palpable, shattering their world in an instant.

"No! God, no!" She screamed to the heavens, her cry echoing the depths of her soul. "I don't believe it." The pain in her voice was proof of the depth of her loss.

She fell to the ground, tears flooding the floor around her, and she cried out,

"My son, my son, my only son. Why? Why? Why?"

She wrapped her arms around her chest, hugging herself, and rocked back and forth. Her husband crouched beside her, trying to offer comfort. But she could not be consoled. Her grief was a force that could not be tamed.

Her only son was dead.

I still have little memory of the day I found out my son died by suicide.

I know the police came. Isabel, my daughter and Sebastian's younger sister by two years, heard the urgent knock around midnight. Opening the door, she saw two blue-uniformed men on the front porch.

"Momma! Papa! Wake up! The police are here."

When I heard her frightened screams and struggled out of my sheets, somehow I already knew in my heart what had happened.

Sebastian was dead.

My husband Steve remembered the police chaplain coming into the house and telling us our son had died in an accident. Sebastian had fallen from a steep cliff.

It was no accident.

Even after eight years, everything else remains a blur.

I know I sent texts to our closest friends to tell them what had happened. I couldn't call. People started coming throughout the night and into the morning. Our pastor, Matt, arrived soon after we contacted him. Matt had visited us in the hospital the day Sebastian was born.

Friends brought us drinks from Starbucks. Steve said they came into the house, stayed for a while, and prayed with us. I remember bodies but not faces.

Over the next few weeks, people continued to stop by. Meals were left on the doorstep, cards were sent, and beautiful plants and flowers were delivered. The outpouring of love and support from our community was overwhelming and deeply comforting. It became a reminder that we were not alone in our grief.

I'm sure Judas' mother must have been enormously proud of her son. She had heard stories about Jesus, a man from Galilee who was a former carpenter and had been performing miracles, including healing the sick and casting out demons. The news about Jesus had been spreading around the countryside. Jesus had even taught in the local synagogue, as if he were a rabbi, and everyone was praising the great things he was saying and doing. I can't help but wonder if she, like me, had moments of doubt and fear, despite the miracles she had heard about.

Then, for Judas' mother, the most wonderful thing happened. This Jesus had handpicked Judas to be one of his followers.

"Mom, Jesus put me in charge of the finances."

Judas' mom probably clapped her hands with pride at her son's accomplishments.

"Better you than that Matthew fellow. I can't believe Jesus picked a tax collector to join your group."

Jesus called twelve men to be his apostles. They followed Jesus around, watching Him do strange and wondrous things. After a while, Jesus gave extraordinary powers to Judas and the rest of Jesus' followers to drive out demons and to cure diseases and sicknesses. Jesus then sent these men to different villages in Israel and to preach to the Jews that "the kingdom of heaven has come near" (Matthew 10:7).

For three years, Jesus instructed his disciples. These men watched Jesus walk on water, calm storms, feed thousands of people, heal leprosy and blindness, and pray for children brought by parents to be blessed. Judas likely heard Jesus instruct the rich young man to sell all his possessions and give them to the poor, promising that he would then have treasure in heaven.

I wondered if Judas' mother was one of many women who followed Jesus on his final journey from Galilee. She must have spent time alongside the mother of Zebedee's sons. Perhaps they chatted about their boys and gossiped while drawing water at nearby wells or preparing meals for Jesus and his other followers.

Judas' mother may have witnessed, and was probably shocked, when Mrs. Zebedee and her sons James and John demanded that they be allowed to sit at Jesus' right and left hand. These would be positions of prestige and power when Jesus came into his kingdom. They all thought Jesus was going to storm Jerusalem and become Israel's long-awaited Messiah. They wanted to secure the best positions once he came into power.

However, Jesus said to Mrs. Zebedee and her sons that they didn't know what they were asking. The Bible reported that the rest of the disciples, including Judas, were outraged by this request. Jesus told them, "...whoever wants to become great among you must be your servant, and whoever wants to be first must be your slave—just as the Son of Man did not come to be served, but to serve, and to give his life as a ransom for many" (Matthew 20:26–28).

In the midst of this drama, Jesus kept reminding his disciples that he was going to Jerusalem to die. He was to suffer many things and be betrayed, condemned to death, and be crucified.

Meanwhile, Judas had snuck away and went to the chief priests, offering to help arrest Jesus in exchange for money. They agreed, and Judas waited for the right moment to betray his friend.

"What do you mean, Sebastian has been stealing from you? He wouldn't do that." I had gotten off the phone with a beloved family member, who had given me bad news.

A few months earlier, Sebastian had been offered a place to live in another state. A new beginning. He hadn't been doing well at home. Now it seemed he was not doing well there either.

Less than a year earlier, Sebastian had left for college, where he had an academic scholarship and had played goalie for his college soccer team.

When he came home from college for Christmas break, he announced, "I'm not going back to school in January." He never told us why or what had happened.

Sebastian enrolled at the local community college and found a job, but he became moodier; he had started smoking marijuana. Marijuana became legal in Washington state in 2012.

We tried to help him and even got him into counseling, but things kept getting worse. My husband wanted Sebastian out of the house. I wanted to give him a second chance.

Then a third chance.

Then a fourth chance.

Then a fifth chance.

I began getting overdraft notices from the bank. I always had enough money in my account. Who could be taking money from my account?

I approached Sebastian when he arrived home that evening.

"Hey, have you been using my ATM card recently?"

Without hesitation or remorse, Sebastian looked me in the eye and said, "Yeah, I have. Maybe you should change your PIN number."

I've heard it said that mothers always believe the best about their sons, even when they do awful things. But when Sebastian looked at me and said what he had done like it was no big deal, my heart broke in a way I didn't know was possible. How could he do this to me, his own mother?

My husband commented to our counselor a few months later, "I knew it was bad when his mother told Sebastian to move out. She couldn't trust him anymore."

My son had betrayed me, but he was no Judas.

Eventually, he moved out of state and lived with an extended family member who offered him another chance.

Then I got the phone call, saying they were sure Sebastian was stealing from them to buy marijuana.

"We wanted to talk to you and Steve first. I think we need to have him arrested."

I was devastated. How could Sebastian keep doing this over and over again?

Steve and I looked at each other, and he told them, "You need to have him arrested."

We didn't know what else to do.

As Sebastian's story reached one of its lowest points with his arrest and time in jail, I couldn't help but feel the weight of heartbreak and betrayal. It was in that moment of despair that my thoughts turned back to another story of betrayal, which felt strangely close to my own experience.

Similarly, as Sebastian was arrested and placed in jail, Jesus too was arrested. Rumors swirled that one of his closest followers had betrayed Him. He was taken in the darkness of an olive grove across from the Kidron Valley, bound by a crowd of soldiers and Jewish officials, and led away to the high priest. The sting of betrayal and the sorrow of watching a loved one make a stupid choice are feelings that transcend time, linking my story with that of Judas' mother in ways I never expected.

Judas' mother must have heard the shocking news of Jesus' arrest. What was even more astonishing to her ears was the fact that her son was the person who betrayed Jesus.

"No!" She must have protested. "Not my Judas. He's a good man." But in her heart, she thought, "How could he do this to me?"

She may have previously heard rumors that her son had stolen from the disciple's cash box. He had even once complained to Jesus about a woman pouring expensive perfume on Jesus' feet and then wiping his feet with her hair.

"Jesus, what a waste of money. That bottle of perfume could have fed a village for an entire year!"

Jesus told Judas to leave her alone. She was using that perfume for his upcoming burial.

Judas' mother may have heard all this gossip from the other women helping Jesus and his followers. She struggled to believe that her son was a traitor who would sell out his teacher for a few pieces of silver.

"Judas wouldn't betray Jesus. Judas loved Jesus. He recently celebrated the Passover Feast with Jesus."

Her son, a traitor?

"I still can't believe it." Judas' mother must have been frantic, looking around, hoping someone else would say it wasn't true, that it was someone besides her son.

The disciples who were with Judas and Jesus in the olive grove said, "We saw Judas arrive after we did, with some soldiers and officials from the chief priests."

Another person said, I saw Judas approach Jesus and say, 'Rabbi!' Judas then kissed Jesus on his cheek. Then Jesus was arrested.

"No! Not my son. I have to find my son and ask him myself."

History does not record if Judas saw his mother after he left Jesus. What the Bible does say is that once Judas realized that Jesus was condemned to death because of what he had done, Judas felt remorse and tried to return the silver coins to the chief priests.

"'I have sinned,' he said, 'for I have betrayed innocent blood.' 'What is that to us?' they replied. 'That's your responsibility.' So Judas threw the money into the temple and left. Then he went away and hanged himself" (Matthew 27:4–5).

Life changed in a moment.

The act of suicide is permanent, but the ripples of that final act leave many unanswered questions.

I know Judas' mother asked these same questions I asked in the days, months, and years after we lost our son in this tragic way.

"Why did he do this?"

"Why did he do this to me?"

"Why didn't we see it coming?"

"What could I have done differently?"

"Was I too hard on him, or not hard enough?"

"Why did he want to die?"

We all want to know the precise thing or event that caused the suicide.

I have an idea why my son did what he did. Judas' mother may have had an idea as well. Usually, it stems from multiple factors that come together in a way that leaves the person feeling trapped in a horrible situation they believe they cannot escape.

But at the end of the day, we will never truly know why our child did this.

Eventually, we have to choose to let go of these unanswered questions and move forward, even when it feels impossible. For me, this process was anything but easy. In the aftermath of losing Sebastian, I spent countless nights lying awake, replaying our last conversations and searching for some clue that might explain his pain. The early days of grief were filled with constant "whys" and "what ifs," and I felt isolated by the overwhelming need for answers that seemed forever out of reach (see Chapter 5). There were moments when even simple daily tasks felt overwhelming. It was only by clinging to the promises of Jesus and through the gentle encouragement of friends who sat with me in silence, offering their presence rather than empty words, that I began to sense a glimmer of hope. It took much longer than I ever anticipated, but once I realized that holding to those questions was keeping me back from real healing. I had to release them to God. In doing so, I found the freedom to extend compassion to both myself and others facing similar grief journeys.

This journey of surrender reminds me of Judas' story in a profound way. Comparably, as Judas' mother may never have found all the answers about her son's choices, I, too, had to accept that some things are beyond my understanding. We are encouraged to consider the humanity of those who are often judged or misunderstood, like Judas, and to recognize the pain carried by their mothers and others who loved them. Letting go of our unanswered questions can allow us to see our children, not only through the lens of their final acts, but as a hurting child, shaped by struggles we may never fully comprehend and yet still loved by God.

Judas' mother loved him.

I loved Sebastian.

THOUGHTS TO CONSIDER

1. What is the first thing that comes to your mind when you read the verse at the beginning of this chapter?
2. How does reading this story of Judas make you feel?
3. Have you ever thought that Judas had a mother? A father? Brothers and sisters? How does that change how you look at Judas?
4. How does this chapter change your understanding of mothers whose child died by suicide?
5. Do you wonder, or have you been told, that your child went to hell because they died by suicide? Write down all your thoughts, and try not to edit your feelings.

CHAPTER 4

More Than a Statistic

"Do not put your faith in what statistics say until you have carefully considered what they do not say."[9]

—William Whyte Watt

On September 19, 2017, at the age of twenty-three, my son Sebastian became part of a heartbreaking trend, joining thousands of young people in the United States between the ages of 15 and 24 who have died by suicide. At the time of Sebastian's death, according to the Centers for Disease Control and Prevention (CDC), suicide was the second leading cause of death in this age group. As of

9 Watt, William Whyte. An American Rhetoric. Holt, Rinehart and Winston, 1970.

2023, suicide remains the second leading cause of death among teenagers and young adults in this age group.[10]

Additional data indicate that males have a higher incidence of completed suicides. They also die almost four times more often than females. It seems, that every person I have talked to in the last eight years knows someone who has died by suicide. It has become a worldwide epidemic that, for a time, no one wanted to admit was happening.

Sebastian, like many others before him, had many risk factors that may have contributed to his early death. According to the National Alliance on Mental Illness, one in five adults in the United States has some mental illness, and around 46% of those diagnosed with a mental health condition die by suicide.[11] Sebastian, since high school, suffered with anxiety, depression, and then, as an adult, bipolar disorder. He had been hospitalized twice for suicidal thoughts and had survived one suicide attempt by hanging.

Sebastian had attended a faith-based residential discipleship program whose purpose was to restore hope for those who have a substance use disorder as well as other serious, life-controlling issues. He had been in the program for about six months when he had his first suicide attempt. We hadn't seen this coming. Everything seemed fine; he appeared to be doing well in his program until his disappearance. I'll never forget his appearance after we saw

---

10 "10 Leading Causes of Death, United States: 2023." CDC WISQARS: Web-based Injury Statistics Query and Reporting System, Centers for Disease Control and Prevention, 5 Jan. 2026, wisqars.cdc.gov/pdfs/leading-causes-of-death-by-age-group_2023_508.pdf.

11 "Mental Health by the Numbers." *National Alliance on Mental Illness*, www.nami.org/about-mental-illness/mental-health-by-the-numbers/

him in the emergency room. He seemed to be dehydrated, with cracked lips and sunburned skin. More jarring were the burn marks around his neck, indicative of a rope that he had once tightly secured in place.

Sebastian *had* tried to hang himself, but fortunately for me, the rope had broken.

We had him admitted to a psychiatric hospital, where he was given a provisional diagnosis of bipolar disorder, and he was soon started on some heavy-duty medications. After a two-week hospital stay, Sebastian was eventually discharged.

We thought Sebastian was getting better. He continued with his rehabilitation program, but we were able to move him to another location closer to home in Bend, Oregon. He was able to see a psychiatrist regularly, who could monitor his medications and mood, but then things changed.

Six months later, this time Sebastian died by suicide and broke my heart.

Sebastian was *more* than a statistic.

Sebastian was a son, an older brother, and an athlete. He loved books, movies, and building Legos. He hummed all the time as a child and loved to dress up. He began playing chess with his dad at the age of four and won a national chess championship at the age of nine. He loved to fish and caught his first trout while fishing with his grandfather when he was three years old. He played Little League baseball and tried wrestling in middle school. He played football and soccer in high school. In his senior year, as a goalkeeper, he was selected MVP by the local paper. He even briefly played soccer in college.

My son loved frozen blueberries and would eat them by the handful. At least twice a week, he'd make cheese nachos. He could eat an entire small watermelon, including the rind, in a single sitting. It was not unusual for him to eat five pounds of mashed potatoes and gravy at Thanksgiving.

Sebastian loved *Star Wars*, *Harry Potter*, and *The Lord of the Rings*. He also collected rocks from every part of the world.

He loved asking questions, and he wanted to know everything.

When Sebastian was five, he asked,

"Did Jesus have to ask Jesus in his heart to be saved?"

"How long is infinity?"

"How can Jesus be the Lamb of God and the Good Shepherd?

After perusing through an anatomy book with a cross-sectional view of the heart, he asked,

"Where's the door?"

"The door?" I replied, not understanding.

He persisted, "You know, the door that lets Jesus into your heart?"

I laughed and pointed to the illustration, "There are four 'doors' in the heart; the aortic valve, the pulmonary valve, the tricuspid valve, and the mitral valve." That seemed to satisfy him.

"Thanks, Mom."

Sebastian always called me M.O.M. I would reply and call him S.O.N. I can still hear his deep bass voice calling me that in my head. How I wish he could tell me that in person today.

He smoked "Lucky Brands."

Sebastian loved his sister. When she was a freshman in high school, he warned older high school boys to stay away from her. During spirit week at school one year, they dressed as Angelina Jolie and Brad Pitt, complete with six dolls representing the Jolie-Pitt children.

The world we live in often tries to categorize our children, especially those who have died young and tragically, by assigning them labels such as "victim," "hero," or "statistic." These kinds of categorizations can make it easier for others to process loss, but they also risk reducing a child's life to a single narrative or label. By labeling them, we risk overshadowing their individuality and the unique stories they leave behind.

There are statistics for every cause of death, intentional and unintentional, and while these lists can be helpful, people get wrapped up in the numbers and not the person behind the number. I didn't want my son defined by what he had done, but by who he was to me, his father, his sister, and to those who loved him and those who rooted for and encouraged him as he struggled on his mental health journey.

Most importantly, Sebastian loved Jesus. Sebastian asked Jesus in his heart when he was four years old. At ten, he couldn't wait to be baptized. After he died, and we all struggled with the *whys* and *whats* of how this could have happened,

A few months later, Sebastian's sister, Isabel, found and read his diary, searching for the answers to these unanswered questions. We had stored his belongings in the attic of our home until we were ready to deal with his stuff. I knew he wrote extensively about his struggles and fears in his diaries, but I was afraid to read them; fearful of the answers.

"Don't worry, Mom," Isabel said after I shared my fears, "Sebastian loved Jesus a lot. He's doing better than we are now."

Every child who died by suicide had a unique story beyond the statistic of their death. As we reflect on the lives of those we have lost, it is essential to remember and honor them as individuals, rather than reducing them to mere statistics. Each child's story, with cherished memories, distinct quirks, and meaningful traditions, should be remembered by those who loved them. By writing down these memories and celebrating what made our loved ones special, we keep their memory alive and create a legacy rooted in love and remembrance.

Another suggestion is to record your memories on your phone using your voice or the voices of siblings, spouses, or other family members and friends. These oral histories can then be saved in a file for when you are ready to listen. You may never be prepared; this is perfectly acceptable, as well.

My Sebastian was a beautiful, intelligent, hurting young man who made an unfortunate choice that ended his life prematurely. He was more than a statistic. He was loved by his family and known by Jesus, who welcomed him to his heavenly home. Sebastian is now healed and whole. I look forward to the day I get to see Jesus face to face and see Sebastian smiling, in his new body unmarred by grief and pain. Through sharing my own experiences, with all their rawness and hope, I intend to reassure others that they are not alone. Every life lost to suicide represents more than a statistic; it is the story of a relationship and the memory of a precious soul who mattered deeply to us and to God. Let us remember, celebrate, and cherish these lives, ensuring their stories continue to touch our hearts and inspire others to do the same.

THOUGHTS TO CONSIDER

1. How does the author challenge the idea of viewing individuals who have died by suicide solely as statistics? In what ways does sharing Sebastian's personal story impact your understanding?
2. How does focusing on personal stories and memories, other than statistics, change the way we honor and remember loved ones who have died by suicide?
3. Reflect on the ways Sebastian's personality, interests, and relationships are detailed throughout the chapter. What details of your child's life can you write about, honoring their memory beyond the circumstances of their death?
4. How does the author's faith influence her perspective on grief, loss, and hope? In what ways does spirituality provide comfort or raise questions in the aftermath of suicide?
5. In what ways can sharing and recording memories help families and communities heal after a tragic loss, and what challenges or benefits might arise from this process?

CHAPTER 5

The Laments of "If Only"

"But as for me, afflicted and in pain—may your salvation, God, protect me."
—Psalm 69:29

"'Lord,' Martha said to Jesus, 'if only you had been here, my brother would not have died.'"
—John 11:21

Journal Entry—A Lament; April 2018:

My son died, and my daughter got married, all in seven months. I wanted her to wait a year; she couldn't and/or wouldn't wait. I felt selfish asking her to wait. It was too soon for me. How could she do this to me? I was mourning, I am still mourning. Wasn't she mourning? How could she do that?

Isn't there a rule somewhere that you had to wait a year, tear your clothes, wear a sackcloth, and cry a lot? I'm in a season of crying, and I cry a lot! I can't be happy for her marriage when losing her brother is still too raw. I don't like her husband yet. Someone had the audacity to tell me that when Isabel married Brennan, that wasn't it great, I got a son again? How can someone say that? Don't people think before they speak? I can't replace my son. He's not Sebastian. I don't have a new son now. I'm never going to have a son again. It's not like going to the pound and getting a new puppy. How do you replace 23 years? I've known Brennan for two years.

The verdict is still out on how I feel about him.

Isabel tells me nothing has changed, but everything has changed. She's not my little girl anymore; she's Brennan's wife. She's starting a new life with him, and she has to leave me. This is the way it's supposed to be. This is how it is supposed to happen in an ideal world. Both my children are now gone, one by death, one by marriage, in seven months. I feel the void immensely. I am empty for the moment, not sure what will happen next. I was looking forward to empty nesting, but not like this.

O God, where are you in the midst of all this?

I can't do this by myself. Please help me.

Now.

If only I were there, I could have stopped it.

If only I had known you were struggling.

If only I knew why you did it.

If only I had been a better parent.

If only I hadn't turned off my phone that night.

If only I had let you come home that night.

If I only did more for you.

If only I could have saved you.

If only I could have my old life back.

If only we hadn't argued that night.

If only my love were enough.

The night Sebastian took his life, he asked if he could come home. He had been kicked out of his drug rehabilitation program that day for making poor choices. His struggles with his mental health and the challenges of the program's rules had been ongoing. My husband and I talked with the director, who said Sebastian could move to a homeless shelter in town. Hopefully, after thirty days in the shelter, he'd realize how good his previous program, in reality, was for him. From our perspective, this rehabilitation program had been a lifesaver for Sebastian. He had only three more months to fulfill his year-long commitment, which would enable him to complete his court-ordered obligations and avoid jail time.

Even though I couldn't allow him to return, deep down as a mother, I wished he could be home and protected. I wanted to take care of him, but at twenty-three, he was in a place where he needed to learn to care for himself. People may have disagreed with us, but we felt Sebastian had been instructed and given the tools to help him live a happy and successful life. Sebastian had a supportive therapist and a community of like-minded individuals; he attended group sessions, went to church, worked, and had a loving family.

Still, we knew that sometimes he chose not to engage and use these tools. Sebastian said he understood my decision. He knew I loved him and that I was his biggest fan. No one loved Sebastian more than I did. I visited him weekly and sent him care packages that included all his favorite foods and small, special presents to spur him on and encourage him.

After Sebastian died, I immediately thought, “If only I had let him come home, this wouldn’t have happened.”

Martha, Mary, and Lazarus were close friends of Jesus. Their relationship with Him was built on trust and deep affection, which is why they turned to Him in their time of need, knowing He could help their brother Lazarus in his time of need.

One day, Lazarus got sick. Martha and Mary were considerably concerned, so they sent a message to Jesus to come and visit their brother. They knew Jesus could heal their brother from this dreadful illness. They had probably witnessed Jesus healing the sick and the disabled.

Immediately afterward, Mary and Martha sent word that Lazarus had died. The Bible says that, after receiving the message, Jesus waited a few more days before he and his disciples went to the sisters’ village. By the time they arrived, Lazarus had already been dead for four days.

Both sisters told Jesus, “If you had been here, my brother would not have died” (John 11:21, 32).

I’m sure other thoughts included:

“Why did you wait and not come sooner?”

“Why did you let my brother die?”

"Why weren't you here to heal him?"

"Did you really care for our brother and us?"

For families and friends who have lost loved ones to suicide, the "if only" thoughts can be the most difficult to get through.

Dr. Elisabeth Kubler-Ross's 1969 book introduced the first model for understanding grief, outlining five stages: denial, anger, bargaining, depression, and acceptance. She identified the if-only laments as a regular part of the Bargaining Stage.[12] During this stage of grief, a person usually finds themselves trying to understand past events and often ruminating over specific events before their loved one died, wondering if they had only changed one little thing, that person would not have died.

Death has a way of shattering the carefully built structures of our lives, leaving us to pick up the pieces. Our Western American culture often expects us to have everything neatly organized. As human beings, we have a deep need to understand why things happen. And when the unexpected disrupts our plans, we long to retrace our steps and rebuild what was lost, hoping to restore everything to how it once was. But we can't.

In a similar manner, as the loss experienced by Lazarus's family led them to question and wrestle with the pain of "if only," the story of Job offers another perspective on suffering and grief. Both stories, though separated by

---

12 McMillian Tomasic, Marisa. "The Five Stages of Grief: An Examination of the Kubler-Ross Model." *HealthCentral*, 7 June 2022, www.healthcentral.com/condition/depression/stages-of-grief.

time and circumstance, highlight the deep anguish that comes when our lives are upended by tragedy.

Job was a man who had it all: family, wealth, health, and friends.

Then one day, it was all taken away from him. A natural disaster killed all of Job's children. His cattle were stolen and destroyed, and he soon became sick with sores that covered his whole body. He had lost it all. Job, at first, praised God despite the awful things that had happened to him. His friends were helpful in the beginning by sitting by him in his pain and sorrow. The Bible says they sat with him in silence for seven days (Job 2:13).

One of the best things we can do when someone is grieving is to sit by their side and say nothing.

Really.

Sometimes, choosing silence over offering well-intended but empty platitudes can be one of the most compassionate things we do for someone in the early stages of grief. Quiet presence allows the grieving person the space they need to process their emotions without the added pressure to respond or hide how they truly feel.

Job's *well-meaning* friends then opened their mouths and began offering their opinions on why Job was suffering. They believed Job must have done something to cause these horrible events. They discussed the matter at length and assumed that he must have sinned for these unfortunate situations to have occurred. Haven't we all thought that about someone at some time in our lives?

Tim Keller writes about Job's friends, "Job wouldn't be suffering like this unless he had failed to pray, trust, and obey God in some way. God would never be so unjust as to let all this happen unless Job had done something to deserve it. So if Job wants to be restored, he simply needs to confess all his known sins and get his life straight."[13]

But Job, in all his frustration, cried out to God, "Why did I not perish at birth, and die as I came from the womb" (Job 3:11)?

Like Job, we can ask, "Why am I suffering?" "Why couldn't I change things or control what happened to me?"

Job wanted justice for the wrong done to him, and he wanted God to take account of his involvement in Job's suffering.

We can learn a lot from Job, but most importantly, throughout all his grief, pain, and suffering, Job never turned away from God. "Amid his incomprehension, he clung to God and continued to hope in him.[14]

As Tim Keller again explains, "Through it all, Job never stopped praying. Yes, he complained, but he complained to God. He doubted, but Job shared his doubts with God. He screamed and yelled, but he did it in God's presence. No matter how much agony he was in, he continued to address God. He kept seeking him. And in the end God said Job triumphed."

God never answered Job about the "why" of all these happenings. God reminded Job that God's ways are not man's ways. They are beyond understanding. God wanted

---

13 Keller, Timothy. *Walking with God Through Pain and Suffering.* Penguin Books, 2016.

14 Moo, Douglas J. *James: An Introduction and Commentary.* Inter-Varsity Press, 1985.

Job (and us) to trust Him for who he is, not for what he could or could not do for us. God doesn't owe us an explanation for why he does the things he does. The concept of God is challenging for humans to comprehend, and we often struggle to accept it.

However, we do know we need to trust in the power of the gospel to transform and liberate us from the darkness that comes from dwelling on the "if onlys."

If God is all-knowing and all-powerful, then we must submit to and accept that, on this side of heaven, we may never know the answers to all our unanswered questions; we cannot know everything. We are only able to manage what lies within our own space; we don't have control over what belongs to someone else.

We need to keep bringing all our "if onlys" to God and trust that even if we never know the answer, God is still good. He is just, he cares for us, and he walks with us in our dark places.

Over the last eight years without Sebastian, I have come to realize that I am not God, and I don't always know what God knows. I have experienced many unresolved questions that have persisted throughout this period. There were many moments when I found myself wrestling with the "if onlys," wondering why certain things happened and wishing I could have somehow changed the outcome. During those times, I made a conscious decision to bring my confusion, regret, and pain directly to God in prayer, even when words felt inadequate or raw. Like Job, I poured out my frustration and disappointment, admitting my inability to understand or control the situation.

Instead of distancing myself from God in my sorrow, I tried to remain honest in His presence, following the example of Job and the psalmists. I found comfort in knowing that God could handle my emotions and questions. Over time, this practice reinforced that God was good, even when life felt unfair or confusing. I learned to lean on His character—His justice, His care, and His constant presence with me in dark places—even when I didn't receive the answers I longed for. My grief journey has deepened my faith and given me a quiet confidence that, although I may never fully understand why Sebastian died the way he did, I am never alone in it.

The Psalms are a great place to read about lament and to learn how to lament to God. These passages are filled with words of anguish, anger, doubts, frustrations, and all the realities of life.

The Psalms invite us to lament. We don't have to hide our feelings from God.

- God promises us that he is with us in our pain and suffering:

  "The Lord is close to the brokenhearted
  and saves those who are crushed in spirit" (Psalm 34:18).

- We can come to God in confidence that he will hear us:

  "I sought the Lord, and he answered me;
  he delivered me from all my fears" (Psalm 34:4).

- When we are downcast and disturbed, we can hold on to the promises that remind us to put our hope in God and remember all His marvelous deeds:

"Why, my soul, are you downcast?
Why so disturbed within me?
Put your hope in God,
for I will yet praise him,
my Savior and my God" (Psalm 42:5).

- God promises to hold us up when we are in despair:

  "The Lord upholds all who fall
  and lifts up all who are bowed down" (Psalm 145:14).

- Although this passage isn't from the Psalms, it expresses hope that God remembers us:

  "...he will never leave you nor forsake you" (Deuteronomy 31:6).

Alongside the laments in the Psalms, there are also strong themes pointing to eschatological hope. Eschatology can be defined as the theological study of "last days" (Acts 2:17). For those who are Christians, this can include discussions about the immorality of the soul, the Last Judgement, heaven and hell, and what happens after death.[15]

The Psalms often move from honest expressions of anguish and despair to the anticipation of God's ultimate deliverance and restoration. This eschatological perspective looks beyond present suffering to a future when God, with the return of Jesus, will make all things right once again. This includes ending all sorrow and establishing God's

15 Martin, Ralph P., and Peter H. Davids, editors. *Dictionary of the Later New Testament & Its Developments*. InterVarsity Press, 1997.But

kingdom here on earth (Acts 3:20–21, Revelation 11:15–17; 19:1; 22:5).

We can see an example of this in Psalms 22. Not only does it recount King David's pain when he cries out,

> My God, my God, why have you forsaken me?
> Why are you so far from saving me,
> so far from my cries of anguish?
> My God, I cry out by day, but you do not answer,
> by night, but I find no rest (Psalm 22:1–2).

But it also points forward to resurrection and eternal life, foreshadowing the hope found in Christ's victory over death:

> All the ends of the earth
> will remember and turn to the Lord,
> and all the families of the nations
> will bow down before him,
> for dominion belongs to the Lord
> and he rules over the nations.
> All the rich of the earth will feast and worship;
> all who go down to the dust will kneel before him—
> those who cannot keep themselves alive.
> Posterity will serve him;
> future generations will be told about the Lord.
> They will proclaim his righteousness,
> declaring to a people yet unborn:
> He has done it (Psalm 22:27–31).

The eschatology of the Psalms reassures believers that their grief and questions always have a place before God, and that one day our messy mourning will be transformed into joy, offering hope. Reading the Psalms through this lens allows us to see lament as an act of faith, trusting in God's promises for a future renewal where He wipes away every tear and dwells among His people forever (Revelation 21:4).

Journal Entry—Poem of Lament:

I don't want to hear about someone you know (or didn't know) suicide story.

I don't want to hear how (fill in the blank) died. I don't want to know the details.

I don't want to tell you how my son died (I know you want to know).

I don't want to see you post the national suicide hotline number on your social media page as a token gesture of presumed solidarity, especially during National Suicide Awareness month in September (1-800-273-8255).

I hated that someone posted an article on my Facebook page about a man falling off Smith Rock. Then they posted, "Was this Sebastian?"

I don't want to hear how my new son-in-law is a replacement for my son. My son cannot be replaced.

I don't want to be told that I should be over my grief after the first year (or second year, or third year...)

I don't want to be a token spokesperson for suicide awareness.

Preferably,

I would like to discuss Sebastian at any time.

I do want to be able to cry whenever I want.

I would like you to discuss Sebastian. I want to hear your stories about him.

I do want to remember the good things about my son; he is more than a suicide statistic.

I do want you to know there is no set time to be "over" the death of my son. I will never be "over" it, but the pain does lessen with time.

I do want you to know that I'm ok in the midst of my pain.

Finally,

I do want you to know that God is good in the midst of all my suffering and grieving. He (God) is my present help in times of trouble. He delights in me and delivers me from all my fears.

It is well with my soul.

THOUGHTS TO CONSIDER

1. If you wish, consider writing your own psalm of lament without focusing on style or appearance (look for examples throughout this book).
2. The index includes a list of selected psalms of lament; in my Bible, I have highlighted the verses that stood out to me in blue.
3. Consider praying through the Psalms. If one reads five psalms a day, the entire book can be completed in one month.
4. The Psalms were written by individuals who experienced a range of emotions, such as anger, sadness, grief, and happiness. Reflect on which psalm aligns most closely with your current feelings.
5. Some people find it helpful to write out each psalm daily and record their thoughts and reflections. You may want to try this for a week and see how God begins to comfort you through His words.

CHAPTER 6

Grief Would Be Less Messy If It Were Just Me

"There never was such a goose. Bob said he didn't believe there ever was such a goose cooked. Its tenderness and flavour, size and cheapness, were the themes of universal admiration. Eked out by apple-sauce and mashed potatoes, it was a sufficient dinner for the whole family; indeed, as Mrs. Cratchit said with great delight (surveying one small atom of a bone upon the dish), they hadn't ate it all at last!"[16]

—Charles Dickens

16 Dickens, Charles. *A Christmas Carol*. Books, Inc., 1868.

I was fine until I saw the mashed potatoes, and then we all started crying.

It had been nine weeks—only nine weeks since Sebastian died. I was fumbling my way through this grief fog, unable to see clearly because of the constant tears that would not stop flowing. My life was unexpectedly engulfed by gushing water from the tsunami that hit me when Sebastian took his life and left me tangled in the debris of his death, unable to sort through the pieces of my destroyed life. Steve, my husband, and our daughter, Isabel, were also mourning their son and brother, though decidedly differently from me.

In some ways, mourning would be less messy if other family members were not involved.

After Sebastian died, Steve needed to tell anyone who would listen, in great detail, everything that had happened before and leading up to Sebastian's death. He did it over and over. I couldn't listen; I'd leave the room and pretend he wasn't talking. Steve needed to process what had happened this way.

I have limited memory of the days, weeks, and months after Sebastian died. I don't recall who attended the funeral. We had a guest book with a list of all attendees, allowing me to check who had come easily. But I haven't yet. Steve remembers almost everyone who was there and what they said to us. His memory was surprising because, typically, my husband is like an absent-minded professor. He was always misplacing his keys and could never remember where he left his wallet, phone, and sunscreen. I was amazed by this, for I rarely forgot anything (at least until Sebastian died). Once, I asked Steve, "What part of your brain got you through medical school?" Isabel, on the other hand, wanted to wear Sebastian's clothes; she needed to smell her brother and keep close to him. On our most recent visit together, she was still wearing one of Sebastian's soccer sweatshirts seven years later.

Isabel read Sebastian's diary after he died. I shoved it in a box and put it in the attic. It is still there. Isabel will occasionally ask if I've read it. I tell her no, and we laugh. I know it's in the attic when I'm ready. It's also OK if I never read it.

Not everyone mourns in the same way, and for grieving mothers, it is tough because, as stereotypical nurturers, we tend to put our feelings aside, knowing we can care for those hurting around us. It can get really messy. But recognizing that others won't grieve the same way can be especially frustrating. As I mentioned earlier, Steve needed to speak with everyone. I could have yelled at him and asked him to stop talking, but somehow, I realized this was how he was dealing with his grief after losing Sebastian. Recently, Steve mentioned that he had to tell people everything, but he acknowledged that he knew it was hard for me.

I did not want to celebrate Thanksgiving.

It was the first major holiday after Sebastian's suicide, and I simply wanted the day torn away from November's calendar. Numerous friends had offered to have us over, but I felt awkward. I knew I'd cry the whole time, then I'd feel bad because my friends wouldn't know what to say, and then they'd be uncomfortable, and then they'd probably cry, and then I'd feel worse, and then I'd have to comfort them. I couldn't deal with anything yet.

Getting out of bed every morning was hard enough.

While reviewing my life over the last eight years, I've come to realize that self-imposed isolation early on after a family member dies is a natural and common response to such a horrible situation. In early grief, we feel compelled to hide away, as if somehow believing that this will stop the pain. In some ways, it's easier to help and care for others in their distress. Still, when it's our own suffering, we genuinely believe, in some warped way, that we are helping others by not being a burden and not allowing them to help us. People sincerely want to help those of us who are grieving. But soon, because we've separated ourselves for much too long, these same friends and acquaintances feel helpless about how to help. Eventually, the calls and texts stop. Those of us in mourning try to shove our grief into its separate cardboard box and stuff it way into a dark closet or under the bed, hopefully to be forgotten. But, even in our isolation, grief continues to show up, forcing us to look it in the eye.

We need safe people in our isolation to help us navigate this arduous journey. We need others to speak the truth and show us love. Gently prodding us to move on, even with baby steps. We need to let people in and care for us in our grief. Someone once told me, in the days following Sebastian's death, that if a friend asks me if they could do something for me, like pick up a table I had bought on Facebook Marketplace before Sebastian died, I need to say "yes." This isn't the time to worry about whether we are bothering them or if we "don't want to be a burden" to that friend with their busy lives. People wouldn't ask if they didn't want to help. This advice became one of my lifelines during the darkest days of my grief.

"Let us do the cooking this holiday. The perfect setting for a wonderful Thanksgiving with the whole family."

My eyes perused the advertisement for a two-hour Thanksgiving cruise on the Willamette River provided by Portland Spirit, a Portland-based river cruise company in Oregon. They promised a beautiful holiday cruise, taking in the scenic views of downtown Portland and the surrounding Milwaukie area waterfront. There were promises of a delicious Thanksgiving buffet with a turkey carving station, all the usual holiday foods, tempting desserts, and live piano music.

It sounded perfect.

The best part of the day was that we wouldn't know anyone on the boat, we'd have a table to ourselves, and nobody would feel sorry for us. We could remain anonymous among the festive crowd, finding a safe space to grieve; therefore, I made reservations for our family.

"Stop right here, I need to take your photo!" A chirpy woman, all dressed in black, came trotting up to us with a camera. She smiled brightly and said, "It'll make a great memory." Her enthusiasm was a stark contrast to our subdued mood, but her genuine attempt to bring some joy to our day was not lost on us. We obliged, and her photo did indeed capture a moment of togetherness amidst our grief.

I did not want my photo taken. I didn't want to remember this day; I merely wanted it to be over. My eyes were in a perpetual state of swollenness from all the crying

I'd been doing the last nine weeks. Didn't she know we were mourning?

"It'll be OK." Steve gently said, as if reading my mind. "She doesn't know."

"Stand behind this buoy," Miss Chirpy, twenty-something, pointed to the white ring beside a railing that kept passengers from falling into the freezing water below.

"Come on, Mom, you stand next to me." Isabel pulled me closer. Dressed in a cute skirt and a heather-colored sweater, wearing her Birkenstocks without socks, we shivered together, our arms around each other in a vice grip, and forced our faces into fake smiles.

Our teeth chattering, we stared at the camera and muttered the obligatory, "Happy Thanksgiving."

"You guys look absolutely happy," our photographer gushed.

Little did she know.

As the shutter clicked and our forced smiles were immortalized, I felt the peculiar weight of pretending, the way sorrow can press upon joy like a shadow on sunlight. It struck me that the world around us kept spinning, oblivious to the storm we carried within. Even simple gestures meant to cheer us could brush past the deeper ache we shared—a reminder that grief isn't always visible, and others may not sense its presence lingering quietly between us.

Then it struck me like an unexpected slap to the face that while dealing with my own grief, I forgot that I was still a mother to a surviving child who had lost her brother and a wife whose husband had lost his son. Cousins were missing a lost relative, and grandparents were missing their grandchild.

And yet, life continues to go on, even while we are grieving. We need to be available to those in our immediate family, helping them with their mourning while also encouraging them to move forward. It is not an easy task. But if we don't take care of ourselves, we can't take care of others. That's why I started seeing a grief counselor a year after the first anniversary.

After the first anniversary, it felt like Steve and Isabel "had moved on." They were both busy starting new things, leaving me feeling stuck and left behind. Usually, I have a million projects to work on, and I enjoy starting new things. I had recently completed my doctoral program three months before Sebastian died. I "had" nothing to do, and I felt more lost than ever. For the first time, I had no direction. Meeting with my therapist helped me realize these "lost" feelings and having no direction were common after such a loss. It was good to know I wasn't going crazy; I was right where I was "supposed" to be after Sebastian's death, still grieving.

My husband once commented that after Sebastian died, he soon realized he would have to go through this season of grief and suffering. He couldn't avoid the grief that was coming and that had arrived. We will never be the same again; we will always be hurt, but the pain will eventually lessen once we start living again.

The loss of a loved one can be compared to losing one's arm in an accident. For our family of four, losing Sebastian was like a traumatic amputation, and now there are only three extremities left. Our family had to undergo a lengthy healing process to be fit for a prosthetic foot. However, the fact remains that the original foot is still gone.

C. S. Lewis wrote after the death of his wife,

> And 'Getting over it so soon?' But the words are ambiguous. To say the patient is getting over it after an operation for appendicitis is one thing; after he's had his leg off, it is quite another. After that operation either the wounded stump heals, or the man dies. If it heals, the fierce, continuous pain will stop. Presently he'll get back his strength and be able to stump about on his wooden leg. He has 'got over it.' But he will probably have recurrent pains in the stump all his life, and perhaps pretty bad ones; and he will always be a one-legged man. There will be hardly any moment when he forgets it. Bathing, dressing, sitting down and getting up again, even lying in bed, will all be different. His whole way of life will be changed. All sorts of pleasures and activities that he once took for granted will have to be simply written off. Duties too. At present I am learning to get about on crutches. Perhaps I shall presently be given a wooden leg. But I shall never be a biped again.[17]

In our hearts, we will always be a family of four, but now we wear "prosthetics" to help us move forward. The stump of Sebastian is still attached to us in our memories, through his paintings and his photos, and sometimes the stump still hurts. There is a "phantom pain" that lingers. Phantom pain is a complex phenomenon experienced by individuals who have lost an extremity due to trauma or

---

17 Lewis, C. S. *A Grief Observed.* HarperOne, 2015.

medical interventions. Despite the extremity's absence, a person's brain continues to remember the missing limb in some way; sometimes, this results in discomfort and often severe, sharp pains. Grieving the loss of a family member brings this type of pain and discomfort, for our brains continue to remember, and it continues to hurt long after the limb or loved one is gone.

The Thanksgiving cruise ship had an enormous but spacious dining room, and we were led to our table by yet another black-attired, perpetually happy staff member. The delicious aroma of baked turkey and ham filled our nostrils, evoking memories of past Thanksgiving celebrations. Inside the cabin, traditional holiday decorations splashed with greens and reds covered every available wall and table. White sparkling lights gleamed from the ceiling, reflecting off wine glasses. At the same time, classic pop tunes with a smattering of Christmas carols were played on a grand piano by a gentleman who, mysteriously, looked like Santa Claus in a black felted bowler hat. The twinkling tunes provided quiet background music and a much-needed distraction as we automatically started playing "Name That Tune" with each new musical selection.

Once the vessel was underway, sailing down the Willamette River at a leisurely pace, designated staff escorted each table to peruse the scrumptious banquet buffet filled with every kind of holiday dish imaginable. The three of us each grabbed a warm plate, and we slowly meandered down the buffet line, oohing and aahing over the variety of foods in front of us. As we filled up our plates with turkey, prime rib, and green beans, I suddenly paused when we reached the creamy mashed potatoes. Frozen in place and unable to dish anything else on my plate, I once again remembered Sebastian, and tears filled my eyes. Noticing my distress, Steve tugged on my sweater and gently pushed past the potatoes. He grabbed the serving spoon and placed a large dollop of creamy potatoes on my plate, then on his own.

Sebastian loved mashed potatoes, but my son loved my mashed potatoes even more. Every Thanksgiving, ever since Sebastian tasted his first bite of this American staple, I would peel at least five pounds of potatoes. Sebastian couldn't wait for the heap of creamy starches to pass his way. Sebastian, without hesitation, piled his entire plate with them, creating a deep crater ready for the turkey gravy.

Inevitably, we would hear shouts from his sister, who always sat across the table from Sebastian.

"Hey, you can't eat all the mashed potatoes! Save some for the rest of us."

"There's plenty." Sebastian would jovially reply. Looking at the empty bowl, he'd smile mischievously and happily announce. "Mom, I think we need more mashed potatoes."

God, I missed his grin.

We filled our plates, including the dreaded potatoes, and we hastened through the happy throngs of people, lamenting our return to the festive table.

Surrounded by laughter, singing, clinking glasses, and toasts being declared around us, tears began to run down all our faces. We were remembering Sebastian and his love for mashed potatoes. We wanted him there with us as he filled his plate. We wanted to hear his deep bass voice.

We needed him to be with us, but he would never be with us again.

Looking back, as we isolated ourselves on that Thanksgiving cruise, I remembered we weren't really alone. Sure, happy (mostly) people surrounded us, but God was with us on that boat, sheltering us from our raging storm. Similar to how Jesus calmed the storm on the Sea of Galilee, we found ourselves in a calm and safe space to cry and mourn the loss of our son and brother. Nobody on the cruise saw us crying at the table, and somehow, it made it better.

We began telling funny stories about Sebastian; we laughed and started crying again. There was a little purging of the pain that had long been consuming us. It was nice to have a respite from the reality of death. At the same time, I slowly started to realize that we might be able to get through this day in one piece with our hearts intact, except for the broken piece Sebastian took with him when he entered Jesus' arms.

Eight Thanksgivings have now come and gone since Sebastian left us.

I peeled another five pounds of mashed potatoes in preparation for our close friends, who would arrive in a few hours. Shaving away the brown skins of the Russet spuds, leaving only the white flesh we'd soon consume, I was again reminded of Sebastian's love for mashed potatoes and how much I missed him. The tears came without warning; they did this less often but always unexpectedly, filling my eyes with bittersweet memories.

My grief has lessened over the years; it's not nearly as overwhelming anymore. Grief is like a scar that remains after a past injury has finally healed. In the same way, as an open wound bleeds profusely, likewise, fresh grief bleeds. We can't stop the hemorrhaging of our broken hearts.

But while the wound is gushing copious amounts of blood all over us and we are frantically trying to stop the bleeding, a miracle, unbeknownst to us, has already started. Within seconds, blood cells start clumping together, knitting the wound and protecting it, and eventually, the bleeding stops. Healing has begun, and we didn't even know it. Within days, scabs develop, and over time, scars replace the once-damaged area.

The pain starts to fade as the wound begins to heal.

Scars, like grief, take a long time to heal—longer than we expect. Initially, the scar appears red, swollen, and misshapen. It can be painful when touched or bumped. The healed area can have a limited range of motion, and the replacement tissue is never as strong as the original. Scars never go away; by the same token, grief never really goes away. They are both constant reminders of what happened in the past. But, with God's help, the mended tissue of grief slowly fades with each passing year until you hardly notice it.

God spoke to his people through the prophet Isaiah about a man of sorrows. This man, familiar with suffering and grief, would be despised by the leaders of his day and not be held in high esteem. He'd take on the pain and punishment of the entire world and die for the transgressions of those he loved. This man would bring peace. Isaiah proclaimed, “But he was pierced for our transgressions, he was crushed for our iniquities; the punishment that brought us peace was on him, and by his wounds we are healed” (Isaiah 53:5).

After his resurrection from the dead, Jesus showed Himself to his disciples, and they were overjoyed. Of the eleven followers, only Thomas was missing. Later, when his friends shared the excellent news with Thomas, he didn’t believe that Jesus was indeed alive. Thomas said he needed to see and touch the scars where the nails had pierced Jesus’ hands and feet.

These scars demonstrated to the world that what happened to Jesus was indeed true.

A week later, Jesus showed Himself again to the apostles. He approached Thomas and said, “Put your finger here; see my hands. Reach out your hand and put it into my side. Stop doubting and believe” (John 20:27). Thomas believed when he saw the scars. Jesus said, “...blessed are those who have not seen and yet have believed” (John 20:29).

These same scars declare what Jesus did for me.

God showed His love and compassion to me by sending His Son, Jesus, born at Christmas time as a human baby in Bethlehem. Jesus became like me in every way possible, yet he did not sin. Jesus suffered as I have suffered; therefore, he understands my pain. Jesus did what no one else was able to do: dying on a cross, dying in my place, that I might have peace, healing in my grief, and forgiveness.

Even when I'm crying in my mashed potatoes, God is with me in my messy mourning. When I couldn't sleep at night because my grief felt overwhelming, or when I found an old sock of Sebastian's hidden away under a couch, and the ache that I thought was under control came flooding back in my inmost being. In those moments when I was sobbing quietly over Sebastian's favorite meal that he'd never eat again or clutching my pillow in the darkness, God's presence has never left me. He continues walking alongside me, guiding my steps until my final days on this earth are over. When I pass through the last enemy of this world, death, I will see Jesus face to face, complete with scarred hands and feet. I have this promise from God, "He will wipe every tear from their eyes. There will be no more death or mourning or crying or pain, for the old order of things has passed away" (Revelation 21:4).

THOUGHTS TO CONSIDER

1. How is your style of grieving different from others in your family?
2. In what ways does it affect you when others express grief differently from you do?
3. How can you support others' grief while experiencing your own?
4. Is it wrong to grieve differently?
5. Do you have something in your grief that others think is silly or that they don't understand?

*I still have not traveled to Bend, Oregon, and I prefer to read the ending of a book or learn all the details of a movie in advance so that I am aware of any events such as suicide or other deaths.

CHAPTER 7

Marriages Don't Have to Fail

"You can't see anything properly while your eyes are blurred with tears."[18]
—C. S. Lewis

It was Friday afternoon at Blockbuster. Sebastian and Isabel were frantically pacing back and forth in the family section aisle, trying to decide which movies they would watch that evening. I already had the half-pepperoni, half-cheese pizza sitting in the trunk, waiting to be cooked when we got home.

---

18 Lewis, C. S. *A Grief Observed.* HarperOne, 2015.

While in the check-out lane and after Isabel grabbed a few Warheads to be eaten in the car, Sebastian asked,

"How come you and Dad always go on a date every Friday night? I mean, you've already been married forever."

"Well," I smiled at Sebastian, who was clutching a newly released *The Incredibles* VHS cassette, "Because after you and Isabel grow up and leave home, Dad, I will still be married. We need to keep working on our marriage, even though we've been married forever."

Isabel's eyes widened as if in shock, and she hugged my kneecaps, "I won't ever leave you, Mamma. I'm going to live with you and Papa forever."

Sebastian, who was ten, replied, "I can't wait to leave home and go and live on my own."

We could not have anticipated that, twenty-six years later, our consistent and modest date nights would become a significant factor in sustaining our marriage after Sebastian's passing by suicide.

When Steve and I were engaged, during one of our pre-marriage counseling sessions, our pastor recommended regular date nights after we were married. He impressed upon us the importance of maintaining a regular date after the arrival of any children we might have to help us reconnect and reset as a married couple. Every Friday night, we would often sit in our favorite Mediterranean restaurant, sharing stories and laughter, figuring out how to be parents to our growing children, and praying for them. These weekly dates, seemingly insignificant at the time, would become one of our lifelines in the tragedy that followed.

Not long after Sebastian died, a well-meaning Christian friend, who had been a part of our lives for many years, visited us. In the midst of this intense time of grief, she casually mentioned to Steve and me, "Did you know the divorce rate is high after losing a child to suicide?"

All I kept thinking was, *Why would you say that to us? Was that supposed to be helpful because it wasn't?*

But over the years since our son died, these supposed well-meaning words kept coming back to me, and I wondered, are marriages more at risk after a child dies by suicide or for any other reason?

While I was doing research for this chapter, I kept reading statistics that supposedly reported an 80-90% divorce rate after the loss of a child. As I searched deeper, I discovered that this statistic came from Harriet Schiff's book *The Bereaved Parent*, first published in 1977. She wrote, "Some studies estimate that as high as 90% of all bereaved couples are in serious marital difficulty."[19] She had no citations for this percentage claim in her book, and apparently, no one at the time questioned its authenticity. According to Sandy Fox, "Grief experts challenged the myth. By 1998, they said there was no evidence of higher divorce rates among bereaved parents."[20] In 1999, a self-help group for bereaved parents, called Compassionate Friends, surveyed 14,852 parents who had reported losing a child. It specifically addressed how parents felt after

19 Schiff, Harriet Sarnoff. *The Bereaved Parent.* Penguin Books, 1977.

20 Fox, Sandy. "Divorce Rate among Bereaved." Open to Hope, 2018, www.opentohope.com/divorce-rate-among-bereaved/

hearing or reading about these supposed 80-90% divorce rates. According to Christ et al.,

> The survey found that of those who completed it, 72 percent of parents who were married at the time of their child's death are still married to the same person. The remaining 28 percent included 16 percent in which one spouse had died, and only 12 percent of marriages had ended in divorce. While acknowledging the potential bias in its sample, the conclusion was that the divorce rate among bereaved parents was substantially lower than is often cited.[21]

More recent studies examining divorce rates among couples following the death of a child have produced mixed results when compared to those of married couples in the general population. But glimmers of hope have been reported. According to the systematic research studies by Albuquerque, Pereira, and Narciso:

> In light of the empirical evidence provided by large-scale quantitative studies, we can conclude that the death of a child can in fact lead to marital distress and divorce, and therefore, must be regarded as a serious risk factor for marital dissolution. However, despite the struggles that couples go through, there is also evidence (particularly in the qualitative studies) suggesting that some couples' relationships can be enhanced by their

---

21 Christ, Gregory H., George Bonanno, Ruth Malkinson, and Simon Rubin. "Appendix E: Bereavement Experiences After the Death of a Child." *When Children Die: Improving Palliative and End-of-Life Care for Children and Their Families*, edited by Marilyn J. Field and Richard E. Behrman, National Academies Press, 2003, www.ncbi.nlm.nih.gov/books/NBK220798/.

shared ordeal, contributing to greater cohesion and support within the relationship.[22]

Sebastian's death surprisingly brought Steve's and my marriage closer together. Given that divorce rates may be higher following this type of death, it is worth considering what measures parents can take to safeguard their marriages.

Complications of Grief

The reality of this life is that everyone we love and care about will eventually pass away. We will all eventually discover that not only is mourning painful and sometimes unexpected, but it is also messy. Many times, this kind of grief is expected; a grandparent or older relative passes away, or another family member finally succumbs to cancer or other terminal illness. At other times, grief comes upon us suddenly; an accident or a natural disaster occurs, leading to many unexpected losses.

No matter how a loved one dies, those impacted by the loss usually experience intense feelings of shock, denial, numbness, and intense emotional pain. There is typically a natural progression of grief and emotional distress that gradually lessens after death, eventually leading to some adaptation after the loss and a sense of developing a "new"

---

22 Albuquerque, Sara, M. Pereira, and I. Narciso. "Couple's Relationship After the Death of a Child: A Systematic Review." *Journal of Child and Family Studies*, May 2015, link.springer.com/article/10.1007/s10826-015-0219-2.

normal without that loved one.[23] A majority of people will adapt and move on in life after learning new ways to cope with the most difficult loss.

Grief after a family member dies by suicide may be more complex. Not only are family members dealing with the "normal" aspects of grief, but they may also be suffering from added feelings of shame and isolation from the stigmas surrounding the mode of a loved one's death by suicide.[24]

Complicated Grief

Mental health researchers and therapists often refer to this as complicated grief. It's like a flood that refuses to recede or a storm that seems to go on forever. Complicated grief is a messy mourning response in which this extreme anguish seems endless, causing more discomfort and pain that can intrude upon life's day-to-day activities. This grieving may especially lead mothers to struggle with the reality of their child's death and finding ways to cope with it.[25]

---

[23] Shear, M. Katherine. "Complicated Grief." *The New England Journal of Medicine*, vol. 372, no. 2, 2015, pp. 153–160, doi:10.1056/NEJMcp1315618.

[24] Levi-Belz, Yossi, and Tal Ben-Yaish. "Prolonged Grief Symptoms among Suicide-Loss Survivors: The Contribution of Intrapersonal and Interpersonal Characteristics." International Journal of Environmental Research and Public Health, vol. 19, no. 17, 2022, article 10545, www.mdpi.com/1660-4601/19/17/10545

[25] Young, Ian T., Amanda Iglewicz, and Deanna Glorioso. "Suicide-Bereavement and Complicated Grief." *Dialogues in Clinical Neuroscience*, vol. 14, no. 2, 2012, pp. 177–186.

Complicated grief may include:

- Intense yearning, longing, and sadness, accompanied by insistent thoughts of images of the deceased and a sense of disbelief that death has occurred.
- Focusing on what may have caused the death to occur in the first place and what could have been done to prevent it.
- Intense guilt or anger towards the loved one or others still alive related to the circumstances of the death.
- Avoidance of reminders of the loss is common.
- Feelings of shock, being emotionally numb, and estrangement from others because of the belief that happiness is inextricably tied to the person who died.
- A diminished sense of self or discomfort with a changed social role after a loved one's death.[26]

Studies have also shown that complicated grief after a death by suicide can last up to five to seven years or longer due to the stigma and isolation that often result.[27]

No wonder my well-meaning friend made that statement about couples getting divorced eight years ago. It

---

26 "Fact Sheet: Complicated Grief." *Association for Behavioral and Cognitive Therapists,* https://www.abct.org/wp-content/uploads/2021/03/complicated-grief.pdf.

27 Levi-Belz, Yossi, and Tal Ben-Yaish. "Prolonged Grief Symptoms among Suicide-Loss Survivors: The Contribution of Intrapersonal and Interpersonal Characteristics." *International Journal of Environmental Research and Public Health*, vol. 19, no. 17, 2022, article 10545, www.mdpi.com/1660-4601/19/17/10545

seemed that the odds were against us in finding peace and solidarity during our already complicated grief after losing Sebastian.

But There Is Still Hope

Despite the numerous studies and advice from experts and well-intentioned friends suggesting that marriages may fail, I hold a belief that there is still hope. It is possible to overcome these traumatic, life-changing events with our marriages and relationships remaining strong and intact. In reality, such shared experiences often lead to growth and resilience, strengthening our relationships in the face of adversity.

Shared trauma can surprisingly be a protective factor in the preservation of a marriage or family. Protective factors, such as shared experiences, are characteristics associated with a lower likelihood of adverse outcomes or that mitigate the impact of a risk factor.[28] Knowing that someone "gets" what happened similarly can be helpful and provide a positive influence on a devastating shared experience. This understanding can make you feel less alone in your grief and strengthen your relationships.

Marriages that were already struggling before the death of a family member by suicide may face an increased risk of divorce. This may indeed contribute to its demise unless protective hedges are in place to help protect and maintain a marriage during such times of suffering and grief.

---

28 "Risk Factors, Protective Factors, and Warning Signs." *American Foundation for Suicide Prevention*, afsp.org/risk-factors-protective-factors-and-warning-signs/.

Protective hedges that can help safeguard a marriage during the immense stress and grief following the suicide of a child may include:

- Recognizing that everyone grieves in their unique way.
- Maintaining open lines of communication during times of grief is crucial.
- Developing supportive relationships outside of our marriage.
- Clinging to God in our grief.
- Praying with your spouse every day.

Implementing these safeguards can help couples weather the storms of grief and strengthen their relationship, even in the face of a loss by suicide.

Recently, Steve and I were having dinner with some close friends. They knew and loved Sebastian and grieved his loss as if he were their son. Brad spoke at Sebastian's funeral. We've cried many tears together over the years. We were comfortable discussing Sebastian with them, and they consistently included him in their conversations. This sense of community and shared understanding provided us comfort and support during our most difficult times.

While sharing a dessert, Brad suddenly declared, "I'm incredibly proud of you guys. The last seven years have been the hardest of your life, and yet your marriage is stronger than ever. I've met many couples whose marriages imploded after the death of a child. You guys are an inspiration to us all."

I began to cry, as I always did, whenever we talked about Sebastian. I was flattered by Brad's words, but I knew in my heart that Steve and I could not have survived the past seven years without the support of good friends like them and Jesus. Especially Jesus.

Five Ways to Navigate Grief and Still Stay Married

1. **Recognize that everyone grieves in their unique way.**

After Sebastian died, I wanted and needed to clean out his room immediately. I had to try to purge somehow this devastating pain that I couldn't control.

My husband didn't want to get rid of anything; Steve didn't want to deal with any of it. At the same time, he would tell everyone who asked every detail of what had happened, both before and immediately after Sebastian's death. Steve, in his own grief, was trying to look for clues to see if he could have prevented what had already happened.

Isabel simply wanted to wear all of Sebastian's clothes. She wanted to smell her brother and somehow keep him close to her. She didn't want to let go of anything. Every item Sebastian owned had a story behind it.

I loved visiting Sebastian's grave site at the cemetery. I found comfort there and would pray for my family and friends. Steve avoided the grave site because every time he went, he would cry. Seven years later, Steve still cries, but the grief is not as intense anymore.

Isabel made a list of songs that reminded her of her brother. It's now over six hours long, and she continues to add to it.

Once I realized that not everyone would grieve like me, it permitted me to grieve the way I needed to, not the way I thought I was supposed to. I also wasn't likely to get as angry with my husband and daughter because they weren't grieving like me, but grieving like they needed to grieve.

We need to begin to recognize that we all grieve in different ways; this is key to moving forward in our grief journey.

2. **Maintaining open lines of communication during times of grief is crucial.**

One of the best pieces of advice my pastor gave us when Steve and I were first married was to continue to date. Date night became a priority. We invested in a babysitter who came every Friday night for over four years. Our children loved date night; they got a new movie and pizza every Friday. Date night was invaluable when Sebastian was struggling with addiction and mental health issues. We needed time to debrief and talk about our day and our children.

After Sebastian's death, we continued our date night, but early on in our grief, we did a lot of crying and tried to sort out what happened. It would have been easy to isolate ourselves from each other, but we knew we needed to work through this together.

Our date night continues after thirty-five years of marriage. We still have to prioritize our marriage, even after the devastation of losing our son. We have committed to each other to be together for better or for worse. We encourage each other. At this moment, we are in a better place, but we have tools in place to deal with things when they start to get worse again.

3. Try developing supportive relationships outside of the marriage.

Having a date night is great, but I also needed safe women to talk to. Fortunately, I have a couple of women with whom I have been meeting and praying every other Monday night for over twenty years. They have been a consistent source of encouragement and wisdom. I'm sure I cried every time we met over the course of five years. Yet they have held my arms up when I was tired in my grief, in the same manner as Moses' brother Aaron and friend Hur held up Moses' arms when the Israelites were in an intense battle and thought they might lose (Exodus 17:11).

Steve also has a group of men with whom he meets on a regular basis. He's now in a place where he can encourage them in their struggles. Before Steve lost his son, he tended to be discreet about his personal life. He never wanted to share because he was afraid to look weak or not spiritual enough. But once he returned to his job, he found that more and more men would come up and share their struggles and worries with him. Steve realized he was more approachable to people, especially men, now. These men felt safer sharing their stories with him, and they somehow knew Steve wouldn't judge them for not being able to handle their families. In our community group, men felt safe even to cry. One husband said with tears in his eyes, "I watched how you (Steve) and Jackie share your story about your son and how you couldn't have done it without Jesus. I see you still have hope. I began to realize I could share my story too."

I went to a grief counselor a year after Sebastian died. It was then that I learned that grief doesn't end after a year, but, to be honest, can feel worse (see Chapter 12). The numbness of grief began to wear off, and I started "feeling" again. The feelings of grief were almost as intense as when I first heard Sebastian had died. I'm glad I had a safe place to process all these emerging feelings that surprised me in my second year of grief.

4. **Clinging to God in the midst of grief is crucial to help preserve a marriage.**

I knew going to church was important, but I didn't want to go after Sebastian died. I believed everyone would be looking at me, feeling sorry for me, and pitying me. Looking back, naturally, my friends from church did feel sorry for me, but not out of malice, but because they loved and cared for me. However, I couldn't deal with everything that was happening, and I was afraid everyone would see me cry.

Steve and I began attending the earliest church service, where not many people who knew us would be, and we sat in the second row on the outside aisle, crying the entire worship time. When you sit up front, you can't see anyone behind you. After the service, we immediately ducked out the closet exit and went home. We hid in this corner of the sanctuary for about four years. But after a while, I didn't feel like I had to hide anymore. Our church was gracious and gave us space; they also never forgot us.

It was also hard to read the Bible after Sebastian died. I could only read the laments of the Psalms, and each time I'd cry. Then I began listening to the Bible on my phone while walking my dog in the early morning. I have listened to the entire Bible seven times over the course of seven years. Listening to God's word every day helped bathe my soul in goodness and God's truths, even when I was in such pain and distress. Sometimes, I couldn't remember what I had been hearing, but I knew it was permeating my mind, and I took it to heart. God began healing me and bringing me closer to him.

5. Pray with your spouse every single day.

Steve and I pray together every day before we leave for work. If we can come together, join hands, and pray for even a few moments, this will set our day in the right direction. We pray for our marriage, our family, our daughter, and her husband, and for those who are also in pain and grief. Steve is better at initiating prayer than I am. There were days early on in our grief that I couldn't pray, but Steve would grab my hand and say,

"Let's pray anyway."

As you reflect on your own marriage in the wake of losing a child to suicide, know that the journey through grief is unique for each person and relationship. Allow space for one another's pain and recognize that healing may take a different form for you and your spouse. Clinging to God and supporting each other in prayer can be vital lifelines, even when words or comfort seem impossible. Remember, it is perfectly normal to grieve in your own way and to seek help when you need it. By being gentle with yourselves and each other, and by holding on to hope, your marriage can endure and even deepen through this unimaginable sorrow. You are not alone, and with time, grace, and support, new strength and connection can emerge from your shared grief journey.

THOUGHTS TO CONSIDER

1. Take a moment and observe how different loved ones in your family are grieving. Make a list of the ways family members are grieving that are similar to you and are different.
2. What is something that someone does in their grief that annoys you? Can you look at the way they are grieving from their perspective? Can you allow them space to grieve?
3. If you are married, what are the practices, behaviors, and traditions you have forgotten about in your grief? What can you do to revive these practices and traditions?
4. If you are a Christian, do you have any daily spiritual disciplines in place? If not, what is one thing you might do to help you begin again?
5. Who can you contact for support this week?

SECTION TWO

In The Middle Of The Storm

"One day Jesus said to his disciples, 'Let us go over to the other side of the lake.' So they got into a boat and set out. As they sailed, he fell asleep. A squall came down on the lake, so that the boat was being swamped, and they were in great danger. The disciples went and woke him, saying, 'Master, Master, we're going to drown!' He got up and rebuked the wind and the raging waters; the storm subsided, and all was calm. 'Where is your faith?' he asked his disciples.

In fear and amazement they asked one another, 'Who is this? He commands even the winds and the water, and they obey him.'"

Luke 8:22–25

CHAPTER 8

When Suicide Comes to Church

"O, that this too solid flesh would melt
Thaw and resolve itself into a dew!
Or that the Everlasting had not fixed
His canon 'gainst self-slaughter! O God! God!
How weary, stale, flat and unprofitable,
Seem to me all the uses of this world!"[29]
—William Shakespeare

"You shall not murder."
—Exodus 20:13

[29] Shakespeare, William, *Hamlet,* Edited by Stanley Wells and Gary Taylor, Oxford University Press, 1988.

Planning an unexpected funeral for your dead child will always be difficult. It is a distressing experience marked by intense grief, confusion, and emotional numbness. Our pastor, who was instrumental in making everything happen, arrived around 1:30 in the morning to be with us after Steve called him with the news about Sebastian's death.

The shock of loss makes thinking clearly nearly impossible; my mind was enveloped in an intense fog that blurred everything, leaving each thought sluggish and heavy. The world felt muted, sounds seemed distant, and there was a physical ache pressing down on my chest. Even the simplest routines, like getting dressed or making coffee, became monumental tasks, performed almost mechanically. During this time, as I felt most lost in that fog, our pastor and church community became a guiding light. They dropped everything and immediately stepped in to support our family, standing by us through every step of this challenging and uncharted process. Their presence was a source of strength, helping us navigate the countless tasks needed for the memorial service. Even though, to this day, many of those moments remain fuzzy in my memory.

One of the most challenging tasks was choosing between twenty-five and fifty photos of Sebastian for his memorial service. The thought of sorting through his baby pictures was unbearable, and each image brought a fresh wave of tears. The grief was undeniably raw that all we could do was cry together as a family. Fortunately for us, someone stepped in to help, because, in the end, we had a ten-minute video that beautifully captured Sebastian's brief twenty-three years with us. After the service, people told us that this tribute became one of the most touching moments of the service.

In addition to selecting photos, we also needed to choose songs and hymns, Bible verses, and speakers for the service. Too many decisions! They were all overwhelming, and I still marvel at how Sebastian's sister, Isabel, found the poise and strength to sing "It Is Well With My Soul" at the funeral. The entire process was devastating, but through it all, our church was steadfast, loving, and compassionate as we struggled to make sense of Sebastian's suicide.

In the days, weeks, and months that followed, the compassion we received from God's people was truly remarkable. Members of our church brought meals to our home, raked leaves, did yard work, prayed with us, and sat with us in silence when words failed. Some spent hours helping us sort through Sebastian's belongings, while others offered a shoulder to cry on or sent thoughtful letters and cards to remind us we were not alone. Their presence filled our home with comfort and warmth when we needed it most.

Our church never gave us the impression that they were disappointed in us or questioned our faith about Sebastian's place in heaven because of what had happened. Instead, they surrounded us with acceptance and love, allowing us to grieve openly and honestly. I am forever grateful for the support and kindness we received. We would not be where we are today without our church's unwavering care and compassion.

"I want people to see Jesus at Sebastian's funeral."

These were my first thoughts when our family sat down to make funeral arrangements for our son. There were a couple of things essential to us. We wanted our friends and colleagues from our respective workplaces to be able to attend the service. We therefore asked if the funeral could be held at 5:30 in the afternoon so that those who wanted could participate after they finished their workday.

The second important thing is that this memorial service wouldn't be only about how remarkable Sebastian's life had been. He wasn't perfect. We wanted people to know that Sebastian had faced significant struggles with mental illness and that he died by suicide. Throughout his challenges, Sebastian had the unwavering support of those who loved him; even during his most difficult times, I knew that Sebastian was known and cherished by God. Our aim for Sebastian's service was that those who attended would see God glorified and come to know the hope we all have in following Jesus. Even in our darkest moments, we believed that God's love offers comfort and the promise of renewal, assuring us that no matter how overwhelming life may become, there remains hope in Christ for all who grieve.

What we didn't realize at the time was that our church had broken an unspoken barrier still common in some churches today: the stigma of suicide. They showed us that the church can be a place of comfort and compassion, even in the face of such a tragic loss. Instead of avoiding our pain or letting old biases shape their actions, our church responded to our family with empathy and kindness. Instead of questioning or judging, they offered practical support—helping us plan Sebastian's memorial, preparing meals, mowing our lawn, and surrounding us with prayer. Their actions sent a powerful message: that even when confronted with tragedy and complicated grief, the church can be a safe haven, where broken people are met with empathy and healing in lieu of shame or exclusion.

At a time when many churches might still struggle to address mental health struggles and the realities of suicide, our church set a different example. By refusing to let stigma shape their response, they stood by us and affirmed that our loss and Sebastian's story mattered. Their love reminded us that the heart of the church is not found in perfection or judgment, but in the willingness to walk alongside people in their darkest moments, to offer hope, and to reflect the unconditional love of Jesus. This experience has forever shaped my understanding of what a true Christian community can look like, breaking through barriers that have long kept hurting families at a distance and proving that compassion can triumph over stigma.

Throughout church history, it has been a place of fellowship, community, guidance, and a source of hope and strength for those struggling with life's challenges. Nevertheless, the church is likewise composed of imperfect, wounded individuals who are susceptible to societal pressures and misunderstandings. According to John Potter, "There is little doubt that Christianity has contributed to the stigma of suicide."[30] In the early church, stigmas may have served as a way to maintain order, unity, and moral

30 Potter, John. "Is Suicide the Unforgivable Sin? Understanding Suicide, Stigma, and Salvation through Two Christian Perspectives." Religions, vol. 12, no. 11, 2021, article 987, www.mdpi.com/2077-1444/12/11/987

standards within the community. In the Old Testament book of Leviticus, the Lord commanded Moses not to allow anyone with certain physical defects, disabilities, or infectious illnesses to approach the altar of His sanctuary (Leviticus 21:16–24). Anyone who met these criteria was prohibited from serving as priests and offering sacrifices. Other people were also excluded from the priesthood, including those not of the tribe of Levi and women.

Perhaps, in later years, by assigning certain behaviors or circumstances, such as suicide, mental illness, or other perceived sins as shameful or unacceptable, the early church tried to reinforce shared values and discourage actions it viewed as disruptive or harmful. These stigmas attempted to create clear boundaries between who was considered holy and unholy, fostering a sense of belonging among church members who conformed and setting apart those who did not. Over time, stigmas may have offered a tool to protect the reputation of the church and ensure that its members upheld the teachings and traditions that defined the faith.[31] While these practices may have promoted cohesion and a sense of identity in the early church, they have, nonetheless, unintentionally created barriers for marginalized, hurting people, often leaving individuals who struggled with stigmatized issues feeling isolated or unworthy of compassion and support.

In recent years, the church has begun gradually changing its views on stigmas, especially on how it approaches people who struggle with mental health issues, divorce,

---

31 Mason, Karen. *The Essentials of Suicide Prevention: A Blueprint for Churches*. Cascade Books, 2023.

single parenthood, and same-sex attraction. We have seen many churches starting ministries that specifically target the homeless, single parents, refugees, and immigrants. There has been a positive shift in the church's understanding and acceptance of these issues, and many are working to break down these stigmas that still linger unnecessarily today.

Definition of Stigma: A set of negative and unfair beliefs that a society or group of people has about something. A mark of shame and discredit.[32]

Stigmas make us feel uncomfortable, especially for those of us who grew up in the church. Some stigmas are so deeply ingrained in our sense of being that it is hard for us to recognize fact from fiction. Being raised as a daughter of a single mother who was living with a man, not her husband, I remember the feelings of being less than perfect when I attended church. I endured the constant stares from behind me while sitting in a church service, and I began to believe that I was somewhat lacking, tainted by the association of being my mother's daughter. There was nothing I could do, even if I was the top female student in my Lutheran confirmation class; it didn't matter. I would never be good enough, no matter how hard I tried.

Over the last hundreds of years, particularly in Europe during the 18th and 19th centuries, many churches believed that if a child died by suicide, the parents or the child must have committed some grave wrongdoing, which could reflect poorly on the church community. For example,

32 "Stigma." *Merriam-Webster Dictionary*, Merriam-Webster, 26 Jun. 2025, https://www.merriam-webster.com/dictionary/stigma.

historical records show that families were sometimes denied burial for their loved ones in consecrated church cemeteries, instead, burying them in unmarked graves outside the boundaries of church property.[33] This false set of beliefs, whether intentional or unintentional, continues to influence some church attitudes even today.[34]

At nineteen, without being married, I got pregnant. The unspoken tenet: I had sinned because I had sex outside of marriage; therefore, I was a bad person. I had failed God and the church. People had definite opinions of my sinful life and let me know. There were a few who rallied behind me, but I felt that I was something that had to be dealt with and hidden away. For this reason, those who attended the church wouldn't look bad. This experience had a lasting impact on me, shaping my understanding of the implications of stigmas within the church community.

In the late 1990s, I experienced depression and started taking antidepressant medication. My pastor supported my decision; however, there was an unspoken stigma in the church at that time regarding open discussions about depression and other mental health concerns. There was some unspoken edict that depression was a sign of weakness or that you weren't spiritual enough; perhaps some unspoken sin, or not enough prayer or faith.

---

33 Minois, Georges. *History of Suicide: Voluntary Death in Western Culture*. Translated by Lydia G. Cochrane, Johns Hopkins University Press, 1999.

34 Potter, John. "Is Suicide the Unforgivable Sin? Understanding Suicide, Stigma, and Salvation through Two Christian Perspectives." Religions, vol. 12, no. 11, 2021, article 987, www.mdpi.com/2077-1444/12/11/987

The Lord prompted me to share my depression story with other women. Even though I was scared, I did what I thought he had asked me to do. Afterward, women began coming up to me and sharing their stories of depression and the need for antidepressants. They felt they had someone who was not judging them in their pursuit of mental health.

After Sebastian died, I began hearing stories from other mothers who experienced firsthand the stigma surrounding their child's suicide. Some were told their child was in hell because they had done something wrong, others felt that church members were shunning them in their grief, and they thought they couldn't go to church anymore.

In the early church, leaders like Augustine (354–430 AD) and Thomas Aquinas (1225–1274) strongly condemned suicide, teaching that it violated the commandments and was a grave sin.[35] Their views heavily influenced church policies for centuries, leading to practices such as denying proper burials and spiritual support to those who died by suicide. These teachings profoundly shaped not only church doctrine but also societal attitudes, making it difficult for grieving families to find compassion. Recent church teachings have acknowledged that some early tenets may have been misinterpreted and caused significant harm to family members grieving the loss of a child. Marginalized people who sought help from the church were often judged,

35 "Augustine (354–430) from *The City of God* from *On Free Choice of the Will*." *The Ethics of Suicide Digital Archive*, 21 May 2015, ethicsofsuicide.lib.utah.edu/selections/augustine/.
"Thomas Aquinas (c. 1225–1274) from *Summa Theologiae*: Whether One Is Allowed to Kill Oneself." *The Ethics of Suicide Digital Archive*, 21 May 2015, ethicsofsuicide.lib.utah.edu/selections/thomas-aquinas/.

turned away, or condemned. The effects of these historical attitudes still linger today, usually making it harder for those affected by suicide to find understanding and support within their faith communities.

A child who dies by suicide leaves behind wounded and grieving loved ones who are, at many times, due to guilt, shame, and other false belief systems, often unable to feel connected to the church. This stigma can lead to increased loneliness and isolation, especially for those who already belong to a church body.

God doesn't want us to face our grief alone.

Social attitudes toward suicide may be influenced by religious teachings, personal experiences, or stories such as the account of Judas's death in the New Testament. Interpretations of these sources have contributed to various beliefs about suicide, including the view that those who die by suicide are condemned to hell after death.

Everyone knows someone affected by suicide. Yet despite its widespread impact, conversations about suicide, especially within church communities, are often still shrouded in silence and stigma.

The question of whether a child's death by suicide remains a subject of intense debate.

This practice remains observable in certain Protestant churches today. In a recent 2024 article found on the Gospel Coalition website, the author Erik Raymond, writing about suicide, declared:

> We need to be clear that suicide is a sin because suicide is murder. And murder is a sin. When we commit

suicide, we are taking our life. We are killing ourselves. Not every case of mental health results in suicide, and not every suicide is a case of mental illness. But every act of suicide is murder.[36]

For those seeking compassion and help from the church while mourning the loss of a loved one to suicide, articles and sermons debating whether suicide is a sin can deepen pain and increase feelings of isolation and despair. It is essential to recognize the unique challenges faced by those grieving a loss by suicide and to respond with kindness and understanding. Instead of focusing on theological debates about suicide, churches should prioritize offering comfort, understanding, and a safe space for those who are grieving.

How the Church Can Help Those Affected and Marginalized by Suicide

First, we, as the church, need to recognize that suicide is a mental health issue and not a moral failing. Broken people come to church seeking help for their brokenness. Many people in the church are currently suffering from mental health issues, including suicidal thoughts. Struggling with suicidal thoughts is not a sin. It's a cry for help, and the church needs to step up and champion these broken people. We as a church need to recognize that we have sometimes failed to help those who hurting, we need to confess that we were wrong, and ask God to help make the church a safe place for those who are not like ourselves, but who made

36 Raymond, Erik. "The Suicide Epidemic Deserves Our Attention." *The Gospel Coalition*, 29 Apr. 2024, www.thegospelcoalition.org/blogs/erik-raymond/the-suicide-epidemic-deserves-our-attention/

in the image of God, and as fellow image bearers, hurting people deserve compassion, understanding and support as they navigate these difficult and sometime life changing events.

We must acknowledge this from the rooftops and not be quick to pass judgment on *why* this is happening.

The unspoken stigma surrounding suicide may keep the church from showing care and compassion; the idea that suicide and suicidal thoughts are a sin still permeates some churches today. The silence from the church, combined with its history of not advocating for those who are hurting in this manner, has led many people within the church to avoid seeking help elsewhere. They may seek assistance from secular therapists and counselors, which is great. Still, the church is missing out on an excellent opportunity to help and give hope to these hurting and grieving people by providing exceptional care and showing them the love of Jesus.

All suffering and grieving people need the church's love and compassion.

Secondly, instead of making judgments about those with suicidal thoughts and those who have died by suicide, we need to love those who are broken, hurting, and touched by suicide. We need to walk alongside those who are suffering and realize this will not be a quick fix. It is not our role to fix, but to be available and willing to help. We need to hurt with those who are hurting, and we will rejoice with those who rejoice. When one member of the church is hurting, we are all hurting (1 Corinthians 12:26). As Mason succinctly states, "Moral convictions about suicide need to be balanced with love." She goes on, "How do we do this? We do this by remembering that suicide is not just a moral issue; it is also about psychological suffering."[37]

When people are suffering from suicidal ideations or have lost a loved one to suicide, it is not helpful to debate the moral issues of suicide and its aftermath, even from the pulpit. The Bible mentions suicide at least seven times: Abimelech (Judges 9:53), Samson (Judges 16:29–31), Saul and his armor bearer (1 Samuel 31:3-6), Ahithophel (2 Samuel 17:23), Zimri (1 Kings 16:18), and Judas (Matthew 27:5). The Bible does not shy away from the events of broken people. We will never fully understand why someone makes this choice to end their life. It is not our place to moralize someone in their suffering, or the suffering of loved ones hurt by their loved one's suicide. However, we can examine these biblical texts and then consider how scriptural interpretations may align with Jesus' words to love your neighbor as yourself.

> One of the teachers of the law came and heard them debating. Noticing that Jesus had given them a good answer, he asked him, "Of all the commandments, which is the most important?" "The most important one," answered Jesus, "is this: 'Hear, O Israel: The Lord our God, the Lord is one. Love the Lord your God with all your heart and with all your soul and with all your mind and with all your strength.' The second is this: 'Love your neighbor as yourself.' There is no commandment greater than these" (Mark 12:28–31).

[37] Mason, Karen. *The Essentials of Suicide Prevention: A Blueprint for Churches*. Cascade Books, 2023.

Walking alongside those who are suffering, keeping our mouths shut, and praying provides a powerful physical and mental presence of peace and love that may lead those in not only physical pain and suffering but also spiritual despair to be embraced by the loving arms of Jesus.

Thirdly, we, as the church, have an unparalleled opportunity in the community to provide help, grace, and understanding to those who are broken. We can do this by educating our congregations and providing teaching about mental health issues that include instructions about suicidal thoughts and self-harm. Our churches can offer the congregation and surrounding communities a place of refuge by providing safe support groups and spaces where people can come and talk without fear of judgment or shame.

After Sebastian's memorial service, Steve and I stood and cried for over two hours, greeting and talking with the many people who attended the service. I can barely remember anyone I spoke to. Still, I recall, over and over again, that after each person had offered their condolences, some would go on to say. "You don't remember, but when Johnny was sick, you came and visited me," or "You always helped me when I was hurting." During this time, while these fellow mourners greeted us, the Lord gave me a picture in my mind. It was a picture of the new heaven and new earth in the book of Revelation. As all these people met with us and encouraged us, it was as if God was in that reception hall. God promised in the last book of the Bible that he would wipe every tear from our eyes. He promised us, "... There will be no more death or mourning or crying or pain, for the old order of things has passed away" (Revelation 21:4). It felt like my arms were being supported, similar to how Moses' friends held up his arms during an exhausting battle (Exodus 17:12–13).

The church *can* be a refuge for those hurting from the devastating loss after suicide. Let's help the church be a safe harbor for those who are broken and in need of support during such a catastrophic loss.

THOUGHTS TO CONSIDER

1. What do you immediately think when you hear of someone who has lost a child by suicide?
2. What thoughts or preconceived ideas about suicide have you always thought were true before you lost your child to suicide? How did your views change afterwards?
3. What beliefs about suicide have you been taught by the church, either intentionally or unintentionally?
4. What does your church or the church do well or not do when dealing with suicide?
5. Do you know your church's stance or doctrine on suicide? Do you agree or disagree with what it teaches? It is reasonable not to always agree with everything your church teaches. It is also appropriate to ask questions and seek clarification about confusing teachings of the church.

CHAPTER 9

Surviving All the "Firsts"

"Twas the night before Christmas, when all through the house
Not a creature was stirring, not even a mouse;
The stockings were hung by the chimney with care,
In hopes that St. Nicholas soon would be there."[38]
—Clement Clarke Moore

"What will I do with Sebastian's stocking?"

It felt almost selfish, my mind wandering to Sebastian's Christmas stocking right after his passing. I adored my son, yet here I was, contemplating his stocking.

The day after Thanksgiving means I can start decorating the house and making it beautiful for the Christmas holiday season. Our family traditionally cuts down a tree the

[38] Moore, Clement Clarke. *The Night Before Christmas*. Putnam, 1988.

Sunday after Thanksgiving. Living in the Pacific Northwest typically means putting on raincoats and rainboots and trudging through mud and varying degrees of precipitation in search of the perfect six-foot Noble or Douglas fir that would grace our living room from December until the New Year.

But after Sebastian died, I didn't know what to do anymore. I was still in shock and grief, numb; I was surprised if I changed my clothes. My normally festive demeanor had been shattered. Before Sebastian's death, I had been busily making Christmas presents, and I had Sebastian's ornament ready to place in his stocking.

Now, I didn't know what to do with his stocking.

Could I still hang it up?

What are the rules when someone you love dies suddenly? How do you navigate the familiar, the comforting, the tradition when it's now a painful reminder of what's missing?

I found myself in desperate need of a manual, a guidebook on how to deal with Christmas traditions after a loved one had died. I craved for someone to show me the way, to tell me what was right and what was wrong.

During that confusing and devastating period of my life, I wrote about Sebastian's stocking: *I don't think I can do it. I can't hang up Sebastian's stocking. It scares me, and it hurts too much to look at it now. How sad it is lying empty in its Christmas box. I feel stupid thinking these stupid random things soon after he's gone. Shouldn't I be thinking more noble thoughts, on what, I don't know. I don't know what to think, and yet I can't get these thoughts about his stocking out of my head.*

The Dreaded "Firsts"

When a loved one passes, everything shifts. The traditions, the trips, the little things that made us a family; they all change in an instant. Sometimes, the changes are subtle; they catch you off guard, a stark reminder of the messy nature of grief.

After Sebastian's birth, I discovered a beautiful stocking pattern, and I began knitting him a red, green, and white wool Christmas stocking. The knitted design gave it the appearance of a cozy Irish Aran sweater, which I painstakingly crafted using double-pointed needles. After I had completed the stocking, I sewed his name on the top, weaving each letter into the stitches with red thread.

It was stunning, and I loved that stocking. It was my favorite Christmas decoration.

When Sebastian's sister was born, I lovingly knitted Isabel a matching stocking in the same hues, along with her name. Along came stockings knitted for my husband and me; they looked beautiful together over our fireplace.

For over twenty years, I have hung up these stockings. They are usually the first Christmas decorations put up, and I cherish them. Is it wrong to love something this much? It's not the stockings per se that I loved, but what they represented. They personified our close-knit family, our traditions, our memories; the four of us, complete and together. They reminded me of beautiful Victorian

Christmas cards, idyllic and optimistic for the future. I knew they were only stockings, but they were a symbol of our family's love and togetherness. Life seemed perfect during Christmas, and I somehow felt a sense of completeness. And then the life I had painstakingly knitted into each stocking suddenly became unraveled with Sebastian's death.

The death of any loved one, without us realizing it, resets the calendars of our lives. It is common for people to make statements that include, "That happened before my son died." "That was after my daughter left us." Death becomes the line of demarcation between the past and the present. When someone gets married, has children, or establishes a relationship, a rhythm or circadian cycle governs their life. It is filled with holidays, birthdays, anniversaries, vacations, and uneventful but meaningful days unique to one's family. This March marks the 36th anniversary of my husband and my first date. Nobody else knows this day is special, but us. Nonetheless, it holds meaning for us and has significance, which we celebrate every year.

After your world suddenly crashes and after you have arranged the funeral, burial, or cremation, and you have decided on a headstone, sorted through personal effects, letters, and insurance details, then all of a sudden, you find yourself faced with the first holiday, birthday, anniversary, or other special day. That's when a new kind of panic begins.

During Christmas, it was our family tradition to spend one weekend in December watching the entire *The Lord of the Rings* trilogy. It was a marathon, complete with pizza, jokes, funny stories, and a discussion on our favorite and least favorite parts. It was momentous and quirky for us, and we looked forward to it. But we couldn't watch *The Lord of the Rings* the Christmas after Sebastian died. We couldn't do it without Sebastian. It would never be the same without him.

I told Isabel my horrible thoughts about Sebastian's stocking. Shame overwhelmed me during this type of grief, and once again, I acutely felt that Sebastian had ripped himself out of my life. This void was immense. His empty stocking was a permanent reminder of his absence.

"What should I do?" I asked her.

Isabel, without even a pause, grabbed my hand and squeezed it. "We hang it up.

He's still Sebastian. It'll be hard, but we have to hang it up; it's tradition."

My all-of-a-sudden-grown-up-daughter turned her head and peered at the empty mantel, "It wouldn't look right without it hanging up next to mine."

Therefore, when we took down the Christmas boxes from the attic, Isabel began opening lids, rummaging through each one, oohing and awing over every Christmas ornament and decoration until she finally found our family stockings nestled neatly together, hidden under the tree skirt. She gently pulled out Sebastian's stocking, still looking pristine after twenty-four years of use. With a shaky hand and tears in her eyes, she walked up and hung it on the right side of the mantlepiece. She returned to the box, retrieved her stocking, and placed it next to her brother's.

After Isabel had hung the rest of the stockings and her mission was completed, with tears streaming down her face, my daughter walked over to me, hugged me, and we sobbed together, missing Sebastian.

I wanted to know if next Christmas would be any better. Would the ache of Sebastian's absence ease with time, or would the traditions of our family continue to feel hollow and incomplete without him? As the holiday approached, I hoped that the pain might soften, that perhaps the memories would bring more comfort than sorrow. But as the days drew nearer, I realized that each celebration, every familiar ritual, was a reminder of all that had changed—and that moving forward meant learning to live without Sebastian and to somehow embrace the grief these days now carried.

There is no right or wrong way to celebrate or not celebrate these still-important events that suddenly seem less important. Some people avoid the holidays; they can't celebrate Christmas or Thanksgiving because the pain is overwhelming, and or they feel guilty for being "too happy" shortly after their loved one has died. Others take trips and try to keep busy. For some, it's business as usual. The mantra was, "He or she would want us to still celebrate such and such." What I have concluded is that it doesn't matter what you do as long as you make some plans. Keeping a schedule and maintaining a routine will help us navigate the event effectively.

In the United States, it is nearly impossible to avoid Christmas as Mr. Crank attempted to do in John Grishman's novel, *Skipping Christmas.*[39] We can try to plan something, no matter how small. If we are unable to decide, it would

---

[39] Grisham, John. *Skipping Christmas.* Doubleday, 2001.

be in our best interests to allow others to make plans for us and assist us in getting through the holidays.

Because I love celebrating everything, I needed to "do something" to keep myself busy. I couldn't remember what I did for Christmas the first year after Sebastian died, but I did find pictures on my phone that captured that first winter season. We still went and cut down a tree (I'm sure I cried the whole time, remembering that Sebastian was particularly meticulous about what tree we cut each year). We attended our church's Christmas Eve service (I know I cried the entire time. I'm glad the lights were low). The pictures show that it snowed on that first Christmas Eve without him; this is uncommon for the Pacific Northwest. I recalled thinking the snow was from God, letting us know He was with us in our messy mourning. As a child growing up in Buffalo, New York, it typically snowed from October to May. I didn't like the snow. I'd tell people, "I only want it to snow on Christmas Eve and then have it go away." God knew I needed snow that first Christmas without Sebastian. We were blanketed in the warmth of God's love and mercy that year, and I experienced my heavenly Father's presence through the miracle of that winter wonderland in our backyard.

Some holidays, you think you'll be totally fine, and yet they still can bring long-forgotten memories, which once again can bring more pain and more grief. I thought the first July 4th (ten months after Sebastian died) would be easier. We were invited to a neighbor's house for food and a fireworks display. It was fine until we got to the house. I panicked. Some of these people didn't know our son had died, and we didn't know what to say. We ate and then quietly excused ourselves. Later, we watched the fireworks from our upstairs window, cried and lamented once again that Sebastian had left us.

As previously stated, a family member needs to develop plans during the first year. Or perhaps a trusted friend. I appointed myself because I needed to do something. Everyone in our family was happy with whatever I planned. They were content to go along for the ride. They couldn't begin to think about what to do. For Sebastian's birthday, I took flowers and a big balloon to his grave (I cried then as well). He had turned twenty-four in heaven.

Not everyone will want to do this. A good friend of mine, who also lost her son to suicide, told me she had planned a dinner to celebrate her son's birthday with the rest of the family. It didn't go well. One sibling complained, "Why do we have to celebrate him now that he's gone?" (see Chapter 11).

The first "whatever's" will always be difficult. We want to avoid these special days, not think about them, but they will come anyway. I dreaded every holiday, birthday, and anniversary because it always reminded me that Sebastian was not here. I'd get angry again that he had done this to me, and then I'd pray and try to move on. But once that anniversary, birthday, or favorite holiday has passed, you can breathe once again. It's like the first time you stood in line, waiting to get a seat on the Disney California Adventure Park's *Incredicoaster*. Merely thinking about going on this high-speed ride that includes a 110-foot drop, followed by a giant loop, can be nerve-wracking. You will undoubtedly be nervous and anxious, especially when you hear the screams in the distance. It takes a while to get to the front; you continue to listen to people screaming when it's their turn, and the closer you get, the more anxious you get. Your hands are now sweaty, your heart is racing, and then, finally, it's your turn. You get in, put on your safety harness, and suddenly, you're off, being propelled through the ride. You scream, laugh, yell, and cry, and close your eyes in fear and frustration, and then all of a sudden, scarcely as it started, it's done; the ride is over. You slowly climb out of the car on the launch pad on shaking legs, and then you realize that you made it through the ride, the day, or the event, and it wasn't that bad at all.

This past year was the eighth Christmas without Sebastian on this earth.

Sebastian's stocking still hangs on the mantlepiece, along with a stocking I knitted for Isabel's husband, Brennan. I once tried to give Isabel and Brennan their stockings when they got married and moved to their own place.

Isabel said, "I can't take them. The stockings all need to be together."

Sebastian's untimely death has now become a part of our family's story, but it's not as devastating anymore. We've been adjusting to our "new normal," and I can say we're doing better. We are healing; the scars of Sebastian remain, but now they are a reminder of what happened and that we have moved forward.

Every year has gotten easier; the tears are less frequent, and when they do come, they are not as monumental. We laugh more; we remember funny stories about Sebastian and laugh even more.

I know, without a doubt, the only reason I can celebrate Christmas each year, or any other holiday since Sebastian's death, is because of the hope that has been in me through all my pain, suffering, and grief.

God loved me greatly, so that over two thousand years ago, He made Himself known to a young teenage girl from Nazareth and told her not to be afraid, assuring her that she had found favor with God. She was to give birth to a baby, a son, and call Him Jesus. He would save all people from their sins, and his kingdom would be an everlasting kingdom.

Through all the firsts and the seconds and the thirds, Jesus is enough. He knows our hearts. He sees our pain and bitterness. He cares for us and will walk with us through all these holidays, birthdays, anniversaries, and other insignificant days. He knows when we are up all night, dreading the upcoming day or special event. We can only get through all these firsts, seconds, and thirds with Jesus. We can't do it alone.

Invite Jesus Into the Pain of Those "Firsts"

When facing the pain of "firsts"—the first holiday, birthday, or anniversary after losing a child to suicide, mothers can invite Jesus into their experience in several meaningful ways:

- By speaking openly to Jesus about your pain, fears, and struggles. Share your anger, sadness, and doubts, knowing that He sees your heart and is present with you in every moment.

- By finding comfort and guidance in passages that remind you of God's love, presence, and understanding. Always go to the Psalms. Psalm 34:18 reminds us that "The Lord is close to the brokenhearted" can be comforting.
- By asking Jesus to be with you as you face each day, especially as you approach difficult events. You can pray for strength, peace, and hope, trusting that He will walk alongside you through every "first," "second," and "third."
- By allowing others who share your faith to support you. Sometimes, inviting Jesus in means letting friends or family pray with you, listen to your story, or simply sit with you in silence.
- By honoring your loved one's memory in ways that feel meaningful, such as lighting a candle, sharing stories, or writing a letter (or making a Christmas stocking). Invite Jesus into these moments by asking for His comfort and presence.
- By resting in God's Grace. Remember that healing is a journey that is longer than we think. Give yourself permission to feel what you feel, trusting that Jesus understands your grief and offers compassion, not judgment.

Through all the milestones and ordinary days, I have found that Jesus is enough. Even when the pain feels overwhelming or the night seems endless, we can reach out to Him. He cares deeply for us and promises to walk beside us, offering hope and healing as we move forward, one step at a time. Jesus gave us this promise, "Come to me, all you who are weary and burdened, and I will give you rest" (Matthew 11:28).

Journal Entry—Written on what would have been Sebastian's 29th birthday:

Happy Birthday, Sebastian,

Today would have been your 29th birthday. How I long to celebrate it with you. It's your sixth birthday in heaven, and this year, I'm a little better. The pain of losing you has dulled some, and I can think of you more and more without crying as much. I'm starting to look at your face in the many photographs scattered around the house. They are the same ones I had up before you died. I still avert my eyes as I walk down the stairs by your senior photo from high school. I can barely see your face; your intense blue eyes stare at me from the periphery of my vision. You perfected the "Blue Steel" look, practicing it for hours in front of the bathroom mirror before that photo shoot. You were handsome, and I had many dreams and plans for you.

I'm not mad at you anymore, though I was for a long time. I was extremely angry at what you did to me, to your father, to your sister. I wanted to help you, but I couldn't. I couldn't do anything but love you, pray for you, and be there for you. Every once in a while, if I'm not careful, the anger comes back, and I'm mad all over again. But it doesn't last as long.

I'm getting better; it still hurts, but not as much. It's as if I had been in a car accident and my leg was amputated. I am recovering, but I will always walk with a limp because I will never be the same again. Every day, I am reminded that my leg is gone. Every day, I'm reminded that you are no longer with us. But I am slowly moving forward, limping, but always towards the future.

I love you, Big Guy. Tell Jesus hello for me.

Love, M. O. M.

THOUGHTS TO CONSIDER

1. What steps might you take to help prepare for an upcoming birthday, holiday, anniversary, or other special event?
2. What have you done already that has been helpful?
3. What have you done that might not have been helpful?
4. As you prepare for an upcoming first event, ask Jesus to prepare and walk with you. How might this change the way you approach the upcoming day?
5. How did you feel after "getting through" a significant day or event?

CHAPTER 10

Lies Grieving Mothers Believe

"Suffering tends to make you self-absorbed. If it is seen as mainly about you and your own growth, it will strangle you truly. Instead, we must look at suffering—whatever the proximate causes—as primarily a way to know God better, as an opening for serving, resembling, and drawing near to him as never before."[40]

—Timothy J. Keller

---

40 Keller, Timothy. *Walking With God Through Pain and Suffering.* Penguin Books, 2015.

Journal Entry:

I can't print the family wedding photos yet.

I have many mixed emotions now that the wedding ceremony is over, as I am waiting for the photographer to call Steve and me over for the obligatory "family" photo shoot. I was supposed to be happy; my baby girl married the man of her dreams. Yet, I am still mad, sad, and grieving the premature death of her big brother. I'm angry at Sebastian all over again. He should have been here with us celebrating this day. Instead, as we approach Brennan and Isabel for the "bride's side of the family" photos, I can't help but see that there is a big piece missing. Our family of four is no longer here, and it's a starkly jarring sight. Sebastian's death has ruined this day for me by his eternal absence. I can't be happy for my daughter when he has only been dead for seven months.

And yet, life continues without Sebastian.

I next watched Isabel's husband's family all gather together and play around before it was their turn to be photographed. I hurt even more. They are all there, all together, all the pieces are in place. They all seem to be undeniably happy, and I am still grieving.

I dreaded receiving the proofs after the photographer had completed all her edits. They are all beautiful. She truly captured the wedding day exactly the way my daughter wanted it. And yet again, each family photograph continues to have that large, gaping hole—a vast, empty void —that can never be filled. Each one is a constant reminder of his death and that things will never be the same again for me. No one else will see the hole in these pictures, except me.

I only printed pictures of Isabel and Brennan and put them around the house. They are next to my favorite photos of Sebastian. He looks happy. I can't print the "family" photos yet.

They are still too painful to look at, but one day I will.

In the aftermath of my son's death, I found myself wrestling with a storm of painful emotions and haunting questions. Grief will always have a way of distorting reality, magnifying self-doubt, and planting seeds of guilt, shame, and loneliness. Over time, I realized that many of the thoughts that tormented me were not truths at all, but lies—persistent, destructive beliefs that held me captive and threatened to block my path toward healing and peace. I have seen over the years that these lies are common among mothers and other loved ones who have experienced the profound loss of a child, especially when that loss comes through suicide. Naming and confronting these lies became an essential part of my journey, allowing me to seek comfort, understanding, and ultimately find hope through Jesus. In the sections that follow, I aim to expose these lies, share the truths I've discovered, and encourage others walking a similar path to find freedom from the weight of misplaced blame and isolation.

Lie #1: I wasn't a good enough mother. It was somehow my fault. I didn't know how to be a good mother, let alone a good wife. My family of origin was messy, and whether I liked it or not, I unintentionally brought unresolved issues and complexity into our marriage. Despite my efforts to leave behind specific inherent values and beliefs ingrained in me during my upbringing, they tried to intrude upon and potentially ruin our new and beautiful relationship. However, through years of counseling, participation in numerous support groups, prayer, and guidance from supportive people, including my pastor, I was able to overcome most of these challenges. Ultimately, I married Steve, the man of my dreams, and we embarked on our new life together.

Three years later, our son Sebastian was born. Steve and I were intentional in our child-rearing methods. I wanted none of my family's "bad" traits to be passed down to our children.

We claimed this verse in Deuteronomy 6:4–9:

> Hear, O Israel: The Lord our God, the Lord is one. Love the Lord your God with all your heart and with all your soul and with all your strength. These commandments that I give you today are to be on your hearts. Impress them on your children. Talk about them when you sit at home and when you walk along the road, when you lie down, and when you get up. Tie them as symbols on your hands and bind them on your foreheads. Write them on the doorframes of your houses and on your gates.

I thought we were doing well as parents; we weren't perfect, but we were trying, and then Sebastian killed himself, and I immediately began to blame myself. I remember the days that followed, the endless tears, the sleepless nights, and the overwhelming guilt that consumed me. It was a dark and lonely time, and I felt like I was drowning in my grief.

I must not have been a good enough mother, or this wouldn't have happened.

Truth: It honestly doesn't matter whether we were the "perfect" mom everyone praised or struggled through some tough stuff ourselves. Some of us watched over our kids like hawks, did everything we could—found the best doctors, therapists, counselors, you name it—and it still wasn't enough. Others of us had our own battles, whether that was addiction, money problems, single parenting, or, at most, trying to keep our heads above water. No matter how hard we tried or how much we struggled, we're facing the same heartbreaking reality: our child is gone. Nothing we did or didn't do could have changed it, and that's the hardest thing to accept.

As mothers, we often (or maybe always) blame ourselves. If only we were a better mom. *We should have known this could/would happen.* Throughout our suffering, this feeling of self-blame is a shared experience among most mothers, a painful but common thread that can connect us in our grief. We are not alone in this struggle.

We spent many years caring for our child, so when something devastating happens, like a child ending their own life, we will always think in some way we were a failure.

It was not our fault. This is a truth we must hold onto, even when it feels impossible. We are not responsible for the choices our children make, and we must not bear that burden. It was not our fault.

I received a phone call from a friend whose son had tragically passed away in a pedestrian/car accident. She had always exemplified the qualities of an excellent mother. She maintained her composure, ensured her children achieved good grades, and actively participated in their activities through volunteering. She had dedicated her life to raising her children properly.

"It was my fault." She told me while we were talking about the reason why she had thought he had died.

"How was it your fault?" I gently asked.

"I forgot to tell him to wear his helmet."

Her adult son was twenty-seven years old when he died. She told me that when her son was a child, she had often reminded him to wear his helmet, sometimes repeating it over and over whenever he was riding a bike or in another vehicle that required a helmet. She was a good mother, but sometimes our children make unwise decisions, either impulsively, unconsciously, or in a moment of despair, which may have tragic outcomes.

We may never really know why this happened. But it wasn't our fault. As Rita A. Schulte wrote, "No matter what you *did*, what you *didn't do*, what you knew, or didn't know, it's still not your fault. You know why? Because you're *human* and being human means being subject to limitations. That's why we need God's help."[41]

We all did the best we could with the resources available to us at the time. Most of us read every book on the market, and we research our children's food and sleep patterns. We wanted our children to be safe and happy. There are times when, despite our best efforts, things don't turn out as we hoped, and it isn't always about what we did or didn't do. Our loved ones made choices—such as moving away, taking risks, or making life-changing decisions—that we had no

---

41 Schulte, Rita A. *Surviving Suicide Loss*. Northfield Publishing, 2021.

control over, and those choices affected us and everyone around them. It's essential to remember that we are not responsible for the decisions others make, even when those decisions profoundly affect us.

We can't go back; we somehow have to let go of the self-blame that can hold us hostage from moving forward toward healing and a closer relationship with God. It took me years to realize this, but once I did, I felt a weight lift off my shoulders. I no longer blamed myself, and I had more compassion for my son and the struggles he faced. I hope you can find this peace as well.

Lie #2: No one understands what I'm going through or understands this pain. I am alone in my grief. When facing profound loss, especially one as devastating as the loss of a child by suicide, it can feel as if the world has closed in around you. This unique pain we experience feels intense and often isolating. At the time my son died, I didn't know anyone who had lost a child by suicide. I didn't think anyone understood what I was feeling or thinking. Other friends had lost children to cancer, accidents, and even miscarriages. Still, I felt my grief was different because my loss came suddenly and unexpectedly, leaving me unprepared for the overwhelming sorrow that followed. Even when friends and family offer comfort or share kind words, their attempts seemed insincere and obligatory. The loneliness of this kind of grief can be so devastating that it makes it hard to reach out or believe that anyone else could relate to your experience.

Truth: Death by suicide is the 11th leading cause of death in the United States, according to the American

Foundation for Suicide Prevention.[42] The AFSP reports that it is estimated that in 2022, 1.6 million people attempted suicide. The CDC reports that in 2023, suicide was the **second leading cause of death** of children and adults ages 10-34.[43]

If you lost a child to suicide, you are one of over 49,000 grieving mothers.[44] You are not alone in this type of grief. Every person who has died by suicide has a mother, a wife or husband, a sister or brother, a cousin, perhaps a child, or a friend who is still living. It's unfortunate that, with these stark statistics, due to the lingering stigma around suicide, people often feel alone and do not feel they can get the help and support they desperately need. However, we need to remember that we are part of a community of shared grief. We need to find our safe people to share our grief and lament. We do not have to face our suffering alone. "The Lord is close to the brokenhearted and saves those who are crushed in spirit" (Psalm 34:18).

Even if we *feel* we are all alone in our grief and it appears that no one understands our suffering, we can rest in the fact that God is near us and hears our cries for help. He promises us that he will never leave us or forsake us (Hebrews 13:5). As Tim Keller writes, "All this means that

---

42 "Suicide Statistics." American Foundation for Suicide Prevention, 1 Apr. 2025, afsp.org/suicide-statistics/.

43 "WISQARS Leading Causes of Death Visualization Tool." *Centers for Disease Control and Prevention*, 2023, wisqars.cdc.gov/lcd/.

44 "Suicide Data and Statistics." *Suicide Prevention*, Centers for Disease Control and Prevention, 26 Mar. 2025, www.cdc.gov/suicide/facts/data.html.

even if we cannot feel God in our darkest and most dry times, he is there."[45]

Reaching out may feel daunting, but even a small step toward connection can begin to ease the burden. This journey through grief is not meant to be walked alone. While our pain is real and valid, and while it may feel like we have isolated ourselves in our suffering, we are part of a larger tapestry of people who have endured loss and found ways to keep moving forward. We need to allow ourselves the grace to reach for support and to let others walk beside us in our messy mourning.

Lie #3: My life will never be the same. This lie can be particularly powerful because it takes hold of us in the rawest moments of our grief, convincing us that the pain of our loss has forever shattered any possibility of joy, meaning, or normalcy ever again. When we believe that life will never be the same, it can feel as though all hope is lost and that we are destined to live out our days in a continuous loop of pain and sorrow. This belief can keep us stuck. Early in our grief, we can't imagine a future beyond our current pain. Over time, these lies can resurface and prevent us from seeking support or from allowing others to help us heal.

For those who have lost a child by suicide, this lie is both a reflection of the truth, that life has irrevocably changed, and a distortion that suggests all goodness has been lost with the person we loved. It can amplify feelings of isolation, despair, and helplessness, making it challenging

45 Keller, Timothy. *Walking with God Through Pain and Suffering.* Penguin Books, 2015.

to engage with life or to find purpose in moving forward. It may also cause us to pull away from relationships or to avoid activities that once brought joy, out of fear that happiness would somehow betray our loved one's memory or minimize our loss.

In my own experience, this lie weighed heavily on my heart after losing Sebastian. I could not imagine a future where I wasn't consumed by grief or defined solely by my loss. For a long time, it felt as though I had lost all the color in my world; nothing tasted, sounded, or felt the same. Every milestone and holiday was a reminder that he was missing.

Truth: It *will* not be the same again. But it does not mean that we have to stop living. The longer we live on this earth, the more likely we are to encounter pain, suffering, death, cancer, natural disasters, and accidents. My father-in-law was the oldest of ten children. At nineteen, he joined the Air Force and flew B-17 bombers over Italy during World War II. He lost men and saw lives and countries devastated by war. He outlived his parents and his nine siblings, dying at the age of 93. He went through a lot of suffering in his life. His life changed with every event he encountered. Still, once he encountered Jesus, he was able to encourage others in their losses because of the hope he had in Jesus.

Grief has changed me, but it also gave me a deeper capacity for compassion, a renewed reliance on God, and a longing to support others in their pain. Rejecting the lie did not diminish my loss; it helped me move forward, honoring my son's memory by continuing to live fully, even in the presence of sorrow.

Life happens; good things happen; bad things happen, and grief happens and will continue to happen as long as we are breathing on this earth. Mourning is not only messy, but it can also be a complex and emotionally challenging process. Even though it may take time, healing can occur if we hold onto the hope that lies within us, which can only come from an honest, life-changing relationship with Jesus. Yes, grief can be devastating, and most days, we can't see in front of us because of the rubble of grief caving in and around us. But eventually, the light will once again shine in the darkness as we climb out of the wreckage. The key is to keep moving towards the light, no matter how bumpy the ride is, and not take our eyes off Jesus.

Lie #4: I could have prevented this if I had known (fill in the blank). This lie is especially deceptive because it fosters a relentless cycle of guilt, regret, and self-blame. After losing Sebastian, my husband and I found ourselves constantly replaying the days, months, and years leading up to his death, searching for signs we might have missed or decisions we might have made differently. The weight of believing we could have prevented his suicide if we had only known more, tried harder, or acted sooner became almost unbearable.

Many parents who have lost a child to suicide struggle with similar thoughts, feeling that they somehow failed to protect their loved one. It can manifest as endless questioning, "What if I had asked more questions?" "What if I hadn't sent him to that program?" "What if I had noticed the signs sooner?" This lie makes it difficult to find peace, as it continually suggests that I could have changed the outcome if only I had done something differently.

Truth: I have come to realize that I am not God. I am not all-knowing; I am a finite being. I have limitations. I cannot always know what my children will do.

The first time Sebastian attempted suicide caught me unaware. He was in a voluntary inpatient rehabilitation program for young men with addiction issues when he walked out of his program and tried to hang himself. I had no clue how extremely despondent he was, that he would try to end his own life. After a two-week hospitalization and the start of medication for depression, anxiety, and possibly bipolar disorder, we moved Sebastian to a rehabilitation program closer to the family. I would visit him once every week. I wanted to keep him safe. I kept telling myself that if Sebastian were in a safe place, he would be protected from evil and mean people, as well as possibly himself.

But as his manic episodes became more intense, despite the medications he was on, I became aware, somehow, that Sebastian might try to kill himself again. He might be "safe" for the moment in the hospital, but it didn't mean this "safe" place I tried to create for him could protect him from himself. In my mind, it was no longer a question of "if" but a certainty of "when."

These thoughts then follow up on Lie #1, which suggests that we, as mothers, should somehow possess extra-sensory superpowers, intuitively knowing that our child needs us and that if we only knew what was happening, we could find a way to fix it and make everything better. However, we do not possess any superpowers, no matter what social media tells us. Only God knows what is going on in a person's heart, and He is not obligated to say to us mere mortals why sometimes awful things happen to those we love.

The Bible gives an excellent example of this with the story of Job. Job was a man in the Old Testament who was known for his righteousness and faithfulness to God. Despite living a blameless life, Job experienced immense suffering: he lost his wealth, his children, and his health. Throughout his trials, Job struggled to comprehend why these tragedies had befallen him. But he continued to seek God and remained steadfast in his faith. "At this, Job got up and tore his robe and shaved his head. Then he fell to the ground in worship and said: 'Naked I came from my mother's womb, and naked I will depart. The Lord gave and the Lord has taken away; may the name of the Lord be praised'" (Job 1:20–21). God finally responded to Job's complaints, reminding him of his human limitations and of God's divine wisdom. Although Job never received a direct explanation for his suffering, he learned to trust God's greater plan. "Then Job replied to the Lord: 'I know that you can do all things; no purpose of yours can be thwarted. You asked, "Who is this that obscures my plans without knowledge?" Surely I spoke of things I did not understand, things too wonderful for me to know" (Job 42:1–3).

As Job ultimately recognized, mothers who have experienced the devastating loss of a child to suicide may find some comfort in knowing that they are not alone in their grief; there is support and understanding available, even amidst profound suffering. God is always with us in our pain and messy mourning. He understands our pain, for he, too, lost a child.

In the end, there is no happy ending on this side of heaven (see Lie #2). I would often hear my patients' parents voice their concerns about their child's rash that would not go away or the lingering cough, even after multiple visits with no resolution. They would be worried it was something worse or that we had missed something. Usually, over time, these ailments would go away. Still, sometimes, my patients' conditions became chronic, and they had to learn to adjust to this "new normal." I always tried to reassure my patients that on this side of heaven, we will continue to get sick, have rashes, cough, and, unfortunately, may develop cancer or some other illness, and eventually, we will all die.

The Ultimate Truth: Jesus answered, "I am the way and the truth and the life. No one comes to the Father except through me" (John 14:6). We are never alone in our grief. Knowing and trusting in Jesus can help us distinguish between truth and lies. He promises not to leave us or forsake us (Hebrews 13:5). The Bible assures us that when we die, those who know Jesus will receive new bodies. Similarly, our children are going to have new bodies: perfect skin, no cancer, no mental health issues, only healed bodies, minds, and spirits. I know that when I am face-to-face with Jesus, there will be no more tears, no more pain, and everything will be new.

This promise of the truth is worth knowing because it offers hope even in the midst of overwhelming grief and uncertainty. Recognizing that we are finite beings with limitations and that we cannot foresee or control every outcome relieves us from the crushing burden of guilt and self-blame. The truth reminds us that we are not meant to carry the weight of being all-knowing or all-powerful; only God holds that role.

In this life, this hope comes from understanding that suffering and loss are not always the result of our failures or shortcomings. As illustrated by Job's story, even those who live faithfully can encounter tragedy and unanswered questions. The promise is that while we may never fully understand the reasons behind our pain, God is with us, sharing in our suffering and offering comfort. This assurance allows us to move forward, accept our limitations, and trust that we are not alone or abandoned in our grief.

Ultimately, this truth encourages us to let go of relentless self-blame and seek peace, knowing that Jesus will walk with us through our darkest moments. Jesus can give us the hope that, even without all the answers, we can still find healing in the midst of our messy mourning.

THOUGHTS TO CONSIDER

1. When you can, reflect and compose a list of all the "good things" you did for your child.
2. In retrospect, do you believe there were any actions you could have taken that might have influenced the outcome of your child's passing?
3. Do you feel responsible for your child's death? Take a moment and write down what you may or may not have done to prevent your child's death.
4. Would it provide some reassurance to know that you were not responsible for your child's death?
5. Do you find it hard to let go of not knowing why and trusting God, no matter what?

CHAPTER 11

Death Day Anniversary

"A deathday party?" said Hermione keenly when Harry had changed at last and joined her and Ron in the common room. "I bet there aren't many living people who can say they've been to one of those—it'll be fascinating!
Why would anyone want to celebrate the day they died?" said Ron, who was halfway through his Potions homework and grumpy. "Sounds dead depressing to me." [46]
—J.K. Rowling

"We have to go to City Hall and get a button," I told Steve, grabbing his hand and tugging him through herds of families and dodging overstuffed strollers filled with

[46] Rowling, J. K. *Harry Potter and the Chamber of Secrets.* Scholastic Press, 2000.

already crying children while frantic mothers were trying to get the perfect photo at the floral Mickey Mouse display in front of the Main Street Train Statión. As we rushed under the railroad tracks, through the berm of the left-hand tunnel, the fumes of fresh buttery popcorn and sweet cotton candy permeated my nose, and my heart began to race as I heard the familiar a acapella voices of Disneyland's Dapper Dans singing "While Strolling Through the Park One Day." Isabel and I are wearing our usual Disney headgear of matching red sequined Minnie Mouse ears.

Steve tugged my arm back. "Now, *why* do we have to get a button?"

"Because we are celebrating Sebastian's one-year anniversary here."

The ritual of remembering a family member who has died has a long tradition in the Christian church and can help aid in the grieving process. There is no right or wrong way to grieve and remember a loved one. What seems suitable one year might not be right the following year. "Celebrating" dead loved ones is not as weird or uncomfortable as it sounds. Since time began, people have been remembering loved ones and celebrating their lives. To those of us who live in the "West," grief tends to be done in private; it is likely to be individualized, and there is an unspoken expectation that one must be done with grief after a certain length of time— usually one year. If one is not "done mourning," then there must be something wrong with them or us. Counseling is often recommended to help "get through the grief" if they weren't in therapy already. To those outside the immediate family, the deceased, it seems, is often forgotten; everyone else has moved on with their lives, and those still grieving usually feel guilty for not "being done" with these unresolved emotions when they are told they are supposed to be done.

I remember going to my doctor a year after Sebastian died for an annual physical. We talked about my loss and my grief, which at the time was still intense. I observed in my chart that she had later entered a new diagnosis of "Prolonged Grief." I felt such shame and guilt that I wasn't "done" grieving. I remember the first time I laughed after Sebastian's death and the immediate guilt that followed. It felt like a betrayal to his memory, a sign that I was moving on when I wasn't supposed to.

It's crucial to understand that one is never truly "done" grieving. Grief is a complex and ongoing process that evolves over time. In the United States and other Western countries, if grieving is still ongoing after a year, it's often labeled as "Prolonged Grief Disorder" or "Complicated Grief." However, in many other cultures, it is not considered abnormal if one grieves for an extended period. In reality, it is expected. This cultural difference underscores the fact that grief is not a condition to be 'cured' within a specific timeframe, but a natural response to loss that varies from person to person.

My mother died due to complications of alcoholism and hard living. It was my first experience of what to do after a loved one died. I picked out the clothes my mother would wear in her coffin. It felt like I was buying a new car. I also had to choose her makeup. There was a wake at the funeral home where people who were grieving could visit us and see her body. I still shudder remembering my grandmother taking a photo of Mom's body in the coffin and saying, "This is the best she's looked in a long time." She did look peaceful, unlike when she was alive. After the funeral was over, Gram invited friends and family to her house for a potluck, where everyone enjoyed Mom's leftover whiskey. I thought it was crude to drink Mom's alcohol, but looking back, it was a way for my family to begin processing the loss of their daughter, aunt, sister, cousin, friend, and lover. Many American families' post-funeral celebrations include food and lots of alcohol.

In Hindu culture, family holds great significance, and funeral customs play a central role in honoring the deceased. According to Hindu teachings, the human body is believed to be made up of five elements: earth, air, water, fire, and space. After death, cremation is usually performed within twenty-four hours; the body can return to these natural elements, a process thought to help release the soul for its next phase of existence. Part of this ritual often involves scattering the ashes in a sacred body of water, such as the Ganges River, which is believed to purify the remains and further aid the soul's spiritual journey. Mourning periods traditionally last from ten to thirty days, during which families may observe various rites. On the thirteenth day, a ceremony called *Terahvin* (derived from the Hindi word for "thirteen") is held, marking the formal end of mourning. This ceremony includes prayers and a communal meal shared among family and friends to honor the deceased and offer support to one another. Another key observance is the *shraddha* ceremony, performed on the first anniversary of death and annually thereafter. *Shraddha* is a ritual offering made to honor and express gratitude to departed ancestors, reaffirming the ongoing connection between the living and those who have passed away. While these practices are widely observed, Hindu funeral customs can differ based on region, community, and evolving family traditions. Although cremation is customary, some families may opt for alternative rites depending on their beliefs or circumstances. Overall, these rituals—primarily actions like scattering ashes in sacred waters—reflect a deep spiritual conviction that such acts help guide the soul to peace and support its journey beyond this life.[47]

During a winter trip through the winding, sun-drenched roads of Crete, I was drawn to the miniature churches perched on posts along the roadside—*kandilakia*, as the locals call them.[48] The whitewashed shrines glowed softly in the fading light of dusk, their blue-painted domes and delicate crosses standing out against the rugged landscape. As we slowed near a sharp bend, I noticed the flicker of candlelight through glass windows, casting golden halos upon faded black-and-white portraits tucked inside. Some *kandilakia* overflowed with vibrant artificial flowers. Deep red roses, brilliant yellow marigolds, and sprigs of purple lavender carefully arranged alongside personal tokens: a child's toy, a silver locket, a prayer card.

---

47 "A Comprehensive Guide to Hindu Funeral Traditions." *Asian Indian Funeral Service*, 24 Aug. 2023, www.asianindianfuneralservice.com/blog/blog/a-comprehensive-guide-to-hindu-funeral-traditions.

48 "Kandylakia: History and Traditions of the Roadside Shrines in Greece." *Orthodox City Hermit*, 9 June 2020, orthodoxcityhermit.com/2020/06/09/kandylakia-history-and-traditions-of-the-roadshine-shrines-in-greece/.

The *kandilakia* marked places where someone had died, often in sudden, tragic auto accidents, and served as enduring tributes built by grieving families of this country. Lighting a candle at dusk, tending the flowers, or leaving small mementos was their way of honoring lost loved ones and ensuring that their memory lingered long after the tragic moment. These roadside memorials were not simply solitary reminders but formed part of the island's tapestry, quietly speaking to me with their presence.

We stopped our rental car and stood before one of these kandilakia; I needed to take a photo, so that I wouldn't forget. As I focused my camera, I felt a wave of tenderness and a remembrance of Sebastian. Each shrine told an intimate story of heartbreak and hope, of lives cut short but remembered by those who made these tiny houses. Grief, in this country, was not hidden away but made visible, etched in glass, stone, and candle flame. I was reminded of my own grief and the rituals that helped us carry the weight of Sebastian's absence.

The universal nature of grief becomes palpable, whether in Greece, America, or anywhere else. We all build our shrines, light our candles, and hold close the people we've loved and lost. I found comfort in the knowledge that the act of remembering transcends borders and language, connecting us through the simple act of honoring those whom we have all lost.

Our bodies also often retain memories that the conscious mind tries to suppress or forget. I'd always be sad on and around February 13, and then I'd remember, even though it had been forty years on that day in February, my body remembers; it was the day I found out my mother had died. Even though we sometimes try to avoid an anniversary, our subconscious mind will not forget. This physical manifestation of grief, this involuntary remembrance, is a continual reminder that our loved ones are never truly gone in our hearts.

As the first anniversary approaches, grief may become more intense. You may have thought you were doing well, but then you start crying for no reason; your head might hurt, and you become more irritable, yelling at your family or spouse. You might want to sleep or not sleep at all. Depression may exacerbate around this time. These physical and bodily emotions are to be expected and can be common, but they certainly don't feel normal. Sometimes, you feel worse than the year before, and you might think you are going crazy. Again, this is a common experience discussed by other grieving mothers who have walked before us.

My husband remarked as we approached our son's first anniversary that the anticipation of the upcoming day was harder than the actual day itself.

I love choosing the perfect planning calendar for each new year. Every birthday, anniversary, and other special event is painstakingly written in its designated block. After Sebastian died, I began to write in new blocks. In the October 19 block, I wrote "First Month." On the November calendar, I wrote "Second Month" on the 19th square. Every month for a year, I made a note on the 19th square. On the 19th day of each month, I made it through, I took a black pen and placed a big X to signify its completion. I didn't understand why it was important, but in a small way, I was able to set tangible goals to help me make it through that first horrible year.

As the first anniversary loomed over me as it rapidly approached, I knew one thing for sure. I couldn't be at home on September 19. It seemed irrational at first. Sebastian didn't die in our house (one blessing for us), but the police came that day and let us know he had died.

Therefore, I made plans for us to visit Disneyland.

The second year, I still couldn't stay at home; we planned a trip to New Zealand, where Isabel was living with her husband. It was there that we spread Sebastian's ashes in the mountains where *The Lord of the Rings* was filmed.

As the third anniversary approached, it coincided with the midst of the COVID-19 pandemic. I still had to leave home after being stuck indoors for most of the year. We couldn't see Isabel, and she was in lockdown in New Zealand; therefore, we planned a hiking trip to Glacier National Park in Montana.

By the fourth anniversary, I started feeling like I didn't have to leave home, but then September became our travel month. Instead of dreading the anniversary, we started looking forward to where else we could go as a family. That year, we had free airline tickets, and we flew to London and Scotland, where, unintentionally, we became part of history by attending Queen Elizabeth's funeral in Hyde Park.

Every year, I'd ask Sebastian's sister, who now lived in Phoenix, Arizona,

"Do you want to get together for Sebastian's anniversary?"

"Of course, Mom." And she'd roll her eyes in her annoyed but loving manner. "I'll always want to be with you on Sebastian's Day.

Since then, on subsequent anniversaries, we have returned to Disneyland, taken a road trip to the Redwoods, hiked in Sedona, Arizona, and eaten lunch at the first Sweet Tomatoes restaurant to reopen after the COVID-19 pandemic in Tucson, Arizona. There, we shared funny stories about going to this restaurant as a family. Our eyes continued to fill with tears as we shared stories, but the tears became less frequent as the years passed.

I may never be home on Sebastian's anniversary, and that is entirely understandable after what our family has been through. Every family is different; some will only stay home and not want to go out at all, and some will go to dinner, spend time with family, and watch movies. The important thing is to decide on something, even if it means you plan to stay home and watch a movie. Plans can change, and that's fine. Yes, we need to be flexible, but be together, talk about your loved ones, laugh, cry, and remember; this way, you will never forget as you move on in your grief.

One of the many perks at Disneyland is the complimentary Celebration Buttons. These buttons announce to everyone at the resort that someone is celebrating a first visit or a birthday. I once took Isabel to Disneyland for her 11th birthday. We got her a birthday button at the guest relations desk at City Hall on Main Street, U.S.A. The attentive cast member wrote Isabel's name in big block letters with a black Sharpie, and throughout that day, cast members and visitors would call out, "Happy Birthday, Isabel." It made her birthday even more special.

Guests can also request "I'm Celebrating" buttons for honeymoons, anniversaries, or other significant events that may be honored during their visit to the park. Thus, the reason I dragged Steve towards the unassuming, red-bricked two-story building festooned with traditional early twentieth-century patriotic red, white, and blue pleated fans billowing in the hot California sun.

Steve was nervous. "I'm not sure I want people to know what we are celebrating." He said the word "celebration" while bending the first two fingers on both of his hands, typically used with an air quote.

I was undeterred. I went up to the front desk after waiting for my turn and asked the cast member for Celebration Buttons for the entire family.

"What are you celebrating?" Our unsuspecting cast member asked.

I paused for a moment, suddenly overwhelmed by the enormity of this innocent question.

I cleared my throat and whispered, not wanting anyone in line behind me to hear, "My son died one year ago."

She smiled. "Well, what better place to be than 'The Happiest Place on Earth.' What's your son's name?"

"Sebastian."

I watched as she took her black marker and wrote Sebastian's name on a three-inch-diameter green-colored button with a picture of the character Goofy wearing a party hat while blowing on a party horn. Above Sebastian's name, she wrote "1 Year" and handed me my button while saying, "I'm sorry for your loss." She smiled again and then said, "Many people come here on this type of anniversary. You are not alone."

I smiled in return, holding back the tears that had filled my eyes, and thanked her.

Journal Entry—On the first anniversary of Sebastian's death:

How does someone reflect, memorialize, or dare I say celebrate the passing, loss, or death of someone you love, especially if it's by suicide? I have been thinking about this for the last couple of months as the anniversary of my son's death is rapidly approaching. Do I have to go to the gravesite and put flowers on the marker for no one to see? Do I have to put a paid memorial column in the obituary section of my local paper, lauding and extolling all his extraordinary accomplishments, and never mentioning how he died (no one ever mentions how a person dies in the paper unless they had bravely died after suffering from cancer)? Do I have to write a huge blog or note on Facebook or Instagram telling the world of my suffering heart and how I miss my son and how the world will never be the same with his passing? Do I have to say anything to anyone? Does anyone even care anymore? Does anyone even remember Sebastian anymore? Do I even hang up his Christmas stocking ever again? These are hard questions, and I'm overwhelmed by the enormity of them all.

Today, on the first anniversary of my son's death by suicide, I choose to go to "The Happiest Place on Earth" with my family...

CHAPTER 12

Mourning Can Be Messier the Second Year (and Beyond)

"Her own misery filled her heart—there was no room in it for other people's sorrow."[49]
—George Eliot

Journal Entry:

One year ago today, I held you and hugged you and said goodbye, not knowing that it would be the last time I would ever hold you and hug you and see you alive. We said goodbye, you told me you loved me in your ever "love you mom" low bass voice, and I left you with a hope that for that moment you were safe and would be ok. You said you were doing better

[49] Eliot, George. *Adam Bede,* Butler Brothers, 1888.

and had a plan; a plan I supported, a plan with a future, and that gave me hope once again. You were hopeful at that moment, and I left you in that place, not knowing that I would never see you again.

No one ever told me that grief in the second year would be worse. I thought once I "got" through Sebastian's death day anniversary, I'd start feeling better. But I didn't. I always thought the first year would be the hardest and the second year would get easier. Somewhere in my brain, I had assumed I would be able to "now" move on with my life and that things would be getting better.

During the days and months after Sebastian died, I went through the motions of my day, not feeling much; my goal was to simply get through each hour, the next day, the next anniversary, the next church event, and the next birthday. Once I checked those off my list and entered year two without Sebastian, it was as if all the emotions I held and blocked inside of me came exploding out. Well-meaning friends and family told me that I should be done mourning, but I was still sad. I found my grief was different and sometimes more intense. I felt worse at times; all these new feelings of pain, sorrow, and suffering came bubbling up out of me as if from some unexplored cavern within my broken heart.

Why was this pain still extremely intense at times?

Why wasn't I done grieving?

Why wasn't I feeling better?

During this time, my husband started a new business that kept his mind and days busy. My daughter and her husband moved to New Zealand to work with a mission agency. I felt for the first time in a long while that I had no purpose. I was also grieving the loss of my daughter; all my children had left me that first year. It was then that I decided to see a grief counselor. I needed a safe place to ask these questions and see if I was going crazy or if I was simply still grieving.

In my first year of grieving, I felt like I was in a perpetual fog that, in some ways, insulated me from much of the pain I was experiencing. Looking back, I felt this "fog" was God's way of protecting me and caring for me in the ensuing days and months of that first year. To this day, almost eight years later, my best friends told me they had come to my house the day after Sebastian died; I still can't remember them being there or what I said. By the second year, the fog began to lift; I started remembering things I had forgotten and began noticing the beauty around me in nature. At the same time, intense feelings of sadness would pop up at unexpected times; I hadn't experienced these feelings the previous year. I began to doubt myself and my previous grief journey; I thought I was doing better, and I wondered why this was hard all of a sudden. In actuality, it was hard all along.

In the second year, you begin to wonder and sense that everyone has forgotten your child. You remember, because you will never forget. The people who used to check in may not check in as much, or not anymore, They appear to be going on with their lives and maybe assume that you are as well (because as many caretakers are capable of looking well on the outside, but in the inside, you are dying by the hour) and that you don't need their constant attention. Maybe they are worried they are bothering you or reminding you too much of your loss. Without even thinking about it, you looked forward to those check-ins, and now that they aren't happening, you may feel more lonely and isolated in year two.

As discussed earlier, the emotional toll of isolation and loneliness often intensifies during the second year, resulting in challenges such as professional and work struggles, decreased motivation, and more often difficulties in forming new friendships.

In my first year without Sebastian, many people reached out to offer help, and I began to realize how much I needed support, despite considering myself independent. We accepted offers of beach homes, received meals, and friends helped move Sebastian's clothes to the attic. I also received letters from distant friends assuring us of their prayers.

In the second year, it's harder to ask for help because, as I have written previously, I should have had it all together. Still, when you're coming out of the fog of grief, you sometimes forget what you thought you took for granted. There is a relearning that happens after a child dies, and we find ourselves still needing help navigating new situations and experiences. We tell ourselves we don't want to be a "burden" and that God will help us. He does: "Praise be to the Lord, to God our Savior, who daily bears our burdens" (Psalm 68:19). But at the same time, the Bible also reminds us to "Carry each other's burdens, and in this way, you will fulfill the law of Christ" (Galatians 6:2).

After the first year is over and you feel like maybe you can come up for air after drowning all year long, and you are trying to figure out how you are going to live without your missing child, it starts to dawn on you in year two that your child is never coming back. I kept expecting Sebastian to walk through the door at any moment, thinking this was all a dream, but in the second year, I began to realize that Sebastian would not walk through our front door again.

During the second year, everyone around had moved on. Sebastian's friends were getting married, having children, and buying houses, and it hit me like a brick to the head that these experiences would never happen to Sebastian or, in a way, to me. I would never be a grandparent to Sebastian's offspring, and I would never have the opportunity to know a future daughter-in-law. I'd never sew quilts or buy presents in the same way. These thoughts would spring into my head, usually during the church sermon, and then I'd start crying again and have to hide my face. I didn't want anyone to feel sorry for me.

Mothers tend to be natural caregivers, and as many mothers do, may put aside their grief while they are caring for the grief of their spouse or partner, their surviving children, their deceased child's friends, and perhaps grandparents. It is almost easier to care for others than to attend to our grief, and we may shut it aside while we care for those around us. In a way, we are avoiding the pain that has been thrust upon us as a way to cope with loss, but eventually, it will catch up to us, hopefully sooner than later.

It might seem as though everyone else has moved on, but as caregivers, we often suppress our own grief; instead, we focus on supporting others through their pain, and we neglect our own emotions. When caring for others, we often set aside our own grief to stay strong for them, believing it's our responsibility to hold everyone together. This can leave us feeling unexpectedly overwhelmed once our caregiving role ends, as the grief we've set aside comes bubbling back to life and feels even more intense. I know this happened to me; seeing a grief counselor was incredibly helpful. Talking to my counselor allowed me to process my emotions and reminded me that it is not a burden to ask for help during difficult times. Support can come in many forms, such as counseling, support groups, or simply reaching out to friends, and seeking it is both normal and necessary.

One mantra I repeat to myself and my patients, which I have learned over the course of my nursing career, is, "If you don't talk it out, your body will act it out." Upset stomach, headaches, fatigue, stress eating, not eating, anger, depression, anxiety, the list is endless. Grief will make itself known, even if we don't say anything; our body knows. The body remembers and responds even when we don't want it to (see Chapter 10).

Finding Hope in the Second Year and Beyond

Grief is unique to each person who has lost a child or loved one. There is no one-size-fits-all approach, and every season of grief is unique as well. The first year of grief will not resemble the second, third, or eighth year.

The uncertainty and unfamiliarity of grief can be challenging and seem overwhelming, especially early on in the process. Grief is an unexpected journey that will get easier if we allow ourselves to go through the process and not avoid it. It can be helpful to talk with someone you trust and to allow yourself to feel whatever emotions arise during this time.

In the second year of grief and beyond, we will still need help, and it is entirely appropriate to continue to ask for assistance. Be brave and ask for help. Family and friends cannot read our minds, and even though we feel like they have moved on and forgotten our loved ones, they may need to know that you are not OK and still require assistance or practical help. I have a few friends whom I have met with regularly before and after my son died. For years, they cared for me as I cried (it seemed like all the time). In a recent sermon, one of my pastors told the story of a paralyzed man and his four friends. In the Gospel of Mark, Jesus comments on the faith of these four friends after they made an opening in the roof and lowered their paralyzed friend down through the hole, giving him direct access to Jesus. They hoped Jesus might heal their friend (Mark 2:1–13). My pastor noted that in community, faithful friends provide faith for friends. Sometimes, you get carried by your friends, and sometimes, you are the one who carries them. During these first years of grief, it is appropriate and right to be carried along by others and helped by our friends and families. The time will come when we can do the same for others.

It is essential to find a suicide support group or grief group. Here, you will find your people; they understand, offer tips, reassure you that you are not alone, and guide you through the years ahead (see Chapter 15).

Without realizing it, most of us have slowly been creating or developing coping skills to deal with each stage of grief differently in year two and beyond. It took me a couple of years to look at the pictures of my son that were on our walls. I couldn't take them down (I wouldn't dare), but I could not look at them. I'd avert my eyes as I walked by them. It became a habit, and I didn't have to think about it, but once again, my body knew for me. I also couldn't post my daughter's wedding photos, as Sebastian wasn't in them; it felt like a disservice to his memory (they are up now, but it was in year five). Going back to church was difficult for many years. I "hid" at the eight o'clock service. Since none of my friends or acquaintances attended this service, I chose to sit in the front row, in the furthest corner seat, which is typically avoided during church services. This location allowed me to remain inconspicuous, blending with the dark walls and black curtains. After the last song was over and before the house lights were turned up, I could slip out the side door and disappear into the parking lot.

It was hard seeing my son's friends getting married and having children. I recall a few years ago when I complained to the Lord about this (another one of my laments). God reminded me that Sebastian was good; he was no longer in pain, and God was with him. God challenged me to pray for these young men, their spouses, and their children. They needed prayers to help them mature and grow in their faith so that they'd be good leaders, husbands, pastors, and fathers. Therefore, I began praying for them, and my grief somehow lessened, and God replaced my heart with hope and grace for others.

As we journey through grief, faith and the support of caring individuals intertwine to help us heal. God's guidance provides comfort and direction, while the compassion of friends, family, and counselors offers practical encouragement and understanding. Together, they form a powerful foundation—God's presence lifts our spirits and gives us hope, and the kindness of trusted people gives us strength to keep going, especially when we feel overwhelmed.

In the first year of grief, you might have relied on coping strategies like keeping busy to avoid thinking about your loss, withdrawing from others, or even suppressing your emotions to stay strong for those around you. Over time, these old approaches may lose their effectiveness, leaving you feeling isolated or stuck once again.

As your grief changes in the second year and beyond, consider trying new, practical ways to support your messy mourning. Journaling can help you express and process complex feelings. Joining a grief support group connects you with others who truly understand your journey, while engaging in creative activities—such as painting, music, or gardening—can provide outlets for hope and self-expression.

Moving forward in grief doesn't mean forgetting—it means learning to live alongside loss, supported by faith and community. Allow ourselves to lean on God's wisdom and to reach out to those who care. Asking for help is a sign of strength. With encouragement from both God and trustworthy people, we can find resilience and see signs of healing, remembering that with God, hope is possible, even in the hardest seasons.

THOUGHTS TO CONSIDER

1. If you are in the second year or later of your grief process, in what ways has your experience changed, either positively or negatively?
2. Which coping strategies that were effective early in your grief process have become less helpful, and what do you think has contributed to this change?
3. Have you set aside your own grief while focusing on caring for your family? What steps could be taken to address this?
4. Do you feel a sense of expectation to move past your grief now that the first year has ended?
5. Are there any hesitations regarding seeking assistance if needed? Who is available for you to contact today?

CHAPTER 13

Dodging Hand Grenades

"It is too dangerous for me to put these things into words. I am afraid they might then become gigantic, and I be no longer able to master them."[50]

—Erich Maria Remarque

"So, how many kids do you have?" My unsuspecting new colleague lobbed this verbal hand grenade at me, and I couldn't duck fast enough as it exploded in my face. This was not the first time this seemingly innocent question has been hurled at me these past eight years after Sebastian's death. And each time it gets thrown at me, I try to

50 Remarque, Erich Maria. *All Quiet on the Western Front*. Ballantine Books, 1958.

dodge it differently. At first, I was not sure how to answer this.

What words can adequately convey the depth of my loss?

How do I say it?

Do I owe them an explanation, or is it sufficient to state that I have two children?

Option #1: I had two grown children, and one died.

But then I felt like I had to explain what had happened; everybody seemed to want to know.

And then they wanted details.

I usually wanted to blurt out, "Oh, my son Sebastian committed suicide by jumping off a 250-foot cliff...."

But I fear that my honesty may bring them discomfort, and that thought alone fills me with regret.

Then, there will be that awkward silence.

This awkward silence never goes away.

But somewhere in my grief-worn brain, I believe they secretly want to know all the details of his death. Maybe I'm wrong, but a part of my psyche struggles with the idea that I must somehow be obligated to repeatedly tell all my horrible truths to people I don't know. Or even to those I do know. I know, in some morbid way, I would want to know.

Before Sebastian died, when I would peruse my local daily newspaper while eating breakfast, I'd always read the obituary column and invariably would be drawn to the cause of death of each individual who had recently died. Usually, the paper would recite that the deceased person was surrounded by their loving family as they bravely fought cancer or some other illness. Sometimes, I'd notice the absence of the cause of death; my thoughts would always wander if perhaps it was suicide. Indeed, it could have been an accident, but wouldn't they have mentioned that? The happy faces of those carefully picked out photos from grieving families looking up at me from the newspaper were usually young, and if I googled it long enough, I'd find out suicide was the probable cause of death. I assume loved ones don't want to write that their beloved child died by suicide. The pain of what happened to them prevents families from writing about it.

I couldn't write an obituary for our local paper after Sebastian died. I didn't want people to feel more sorry for me than they already did. If you write about your child dying by suicide, it means it happened, and they are really dead.

Sebastian was really dead.

Option #2: "I have two grown children."

I could leave it at that. But then, my unsuspecting friend will almost always ask the following well-meaning, not intending to hurt me, question, "So, what are they doing now?"

AH!

That won't work. I technically didn't lie. I do have two children; only one died.

Option #3: "I have two children," and then I quickly begin this long diatribe about my daughter's marriage and go into great detail about her dating, engagement, the wedding day, her dress that I altered, hoping, silently praying, my heart beating fast, my palms sweating, that they will forget to ask about my other child who died. This phrase has occasionally worked well for me when meeting new people for the first time.

Option #4: "My kids are all grown and moved out."

However, this leaves room for further questions and potential discussions about Sebastian that I had not been ready to address until recently, and I quickly resort to my stock answer from Option #2. Part of me feels like I'm betraying my son by not talking about him, as I can readily talk about how well his sister is doing. I could talk about what he did before he died, but that would entail mentioning words like rehab, psych hospitals, and a previous suicide attempt. I would have to go back five or six years, before his illness began, to reach the "happy" parts—like the meaningful conversations we would have about music on those long rides together to his soccer practices or the sound of his deep laughter filling the kitchen after one of his father's dad jokes. During those earlier years, my stock answer when someone asked about him was always, "He's doing well today, and he is safe."

Option #5: "I have two children; my happily married daughter and her husband are living

and working in Phoenix, Arizona, and my son is happily living in heaven with Jesus."

There will still be an awkward silence, followed by, "I'm sorry for your loss." I know with certainty that Sebastian is healthy, whole, healed, and safe in the arms of Jesus. I can always talk about Jesus; this gives me hope. I don't want to keep dwelling on what happened in the past; my current life is more than his death by suicide, and Sebastian's new life is more than his death by suicide. He's more alive now than when he was alive on this earth.

None of the options above is perfect, and the longer I mourn Sebastian's death, my gut reaction is not as raw and painful each time this question is asked. Perhaps I am getting accustomed to my new normal, and answering this question is no longer as daunting as it was when I first heard it posed to me. I find I can laugh more and remember funny stories about him again. My thoughts are no longer consumed by what he did, but instead by who he was and is to me now.

The more I talk about my son, the easier it is to tell his story. What I have discovered over the last eight years is that when I share about Sebastian, and I am vulnerable with people about my struggles, I find it becomes easier for people to open up and share their hurts and suffering. Who knew that sharing my pain would allow others to share theirs as well? My grief has given other people glimmers of the hope that is in me, which comes from trusting Jesus to guide me through my messy mourning.

For this reason, when I'm once again assailed by the unsuspecting hand grenade of "How many children do I have?" my "new normal" can talk about him much more freely once again, and though it is not as painful, it's also not as sad as when it first happened. I can live with that, knowing Sebastian is doing well, and I will be alright.

As we move forward in our messy mourning, remember that there is no single "right" way to answer the question, "How many children do you have?" We can choose to respond in whatever way feels most authentic and healing for us in that moment—whether that means sharing openly about our loss, focusing on the joyful memories, or simply saying what makes us comfortable. Allow ourselves the grace to adjust our answer as our grief journey progresses, knowing that our story matters and our feelings are valid. Finding a response that honors both our child and our own well-being can be a meaningful step in embracing our "new normal" and living with hope for the future.

THOUGHTS TO CONSIDER

1. How do you respond to the question "How many children do you have?
2. Recommendation: Prepare a "script" about what you might say when specific questions are asked. People usually mean well when asking personal questions, but they may not realize or understand how difficult it is for the person being asked to answer. How might preparing a "script" for difficult conversations support you in your grief journey?
3. Is it easier to stay home and isolate than risk being hurled with this type of "hand grenade?
4. How have your strategies for handling difficult or explosive questions about your loss evolved? Are there particular responses that have helped you navigate these moments?
5. If you have been on this grief journey for a while, have you found it easier to talk about your deceased child or not? If it is still tricky, why do you think it is? What can you do to make a difference in your life?

SECTION THREE

After The Storm—Grieving With Hope

"Brothers and sisters, we do not want you to be uninformed about those who sleep in death, so that you do not grieve like the rest of mankind, who have no hope. For we believe that Jesus died and rose again, and so we believe that God will bring with Jesus those who have fallen asleep in him...Therefore encourage one another with these words."

1Thessalonians 4:13–14, 18

CHAPTER 14

Losing and Finding Our Identity

"I would rather be what God chose to make me, than the most glorious creature that I could think of. For to have been thought about—born in God's thoughts—and then made by God, is the dearest, grandest, most precious thing in all thinking."[51]
—George MacDonald

"I just want my son back."

"I miss my boy so much."

"Why did he have to die?"

"God, give me my son back."

"Why did this happen to me?"

51 MacDonald, George. *David Elginbrod*. Hurst and Blackett, 1863.

It's been over seven years since I prayed these words and cried my heart to the Lord. But as I meet other mothers who have recently lost a child, especially to suicide, these often-said phrases repeat themselves over and over in our conversations. It becomes a mantra of sorts; if I say it enough, "I want my son back," or wish it enough, it will miraculously come true. Our child would come back somehow from the dead. In these shared moments of grief, we find a connection that transcends words.

The Bible recounts several miraculous instances where mothers experienced the resuscitation of their child from the dead.

In 1 Kings, the prophet Elijah raised the son of the widow of Zarephath from the dead. Elijah had been instrumental in saving this widow and her son from starvation during a severe famine. Later on, when all seemed well, the widow's son suddenly fell ill and died. "She said to Elijah, 'What do you have against me, man of God? Did you come to remind me of all my sin and kill my son?'" (1 Kings 17:18). But Elijah prayed and stretched himself over the widow's son three times, resulting in his miraculous revival. Then the widow said, "Now I know you are a man of God and that the word of the Lord from your mouth is true" (1 Kings 17:24).

Elijah's successor, Elisha, performed a similar miracle for another mother in 2 Kings. This Shunammite woman had no children, and because her husband was old, she'd probably soon be a widow and remain childless. Elisha promised her a son. She didn't want to believe Elisha; she didn't want to hope that this could happen, and yet it did. God gave her a son despite the odds being against her.

But then, one day, this mother's son developed a severe headache and died.

The Shunammite woman was in terrible grief; she was angry with Elisha and grabbed hold of his feet. "Did I ask you for a son, my Lord?" she said. "Didn't I tell you, 'Don't raise my hopes'?" (2 Kings 4:28). But like Elijah, Elisha prayed and stretched himself over the Shunammite's son's body. The boy opened his eyes, alive once more.

While these biblical stories offer comfort and hope through their miracles, they also prod us to reflect more deeply on what it truly means to wish for our child's return, especially when we consider the pain and struggles they endured. If we take the time to think about it, would we really want our child back, especially if they were hurting, self-harming, depressed, and in such a bad place in their mind that caused them to take their life? The horrible pain and suffering they were in that single moment when they lost sight of any hope that might have saved them?

The mommy part of us believes that if we got them back, we could still somehow help them. But we could not. We tend to believe the lie that we had somehow failed our children because they died. We must have/could have/should have done something to help them. But sometimes, we could not. Yet, in the face of this unimaginable loss, we can find strength to carry on, a strength that comes from our faith and the knowledge that we are not alone in our suffering.

Carrying on after the loss of a child, especially to suicide, is a challenging journey, one that can feel impossible at times. While the longing for our child's return never truly fades, finding a way forward begins with acknowledging both the depth of our grief and the love that remains.

First, it is essential to allow ourselves to grieve honestly and thoroughly. Meaning, allowing ourselves permission to grieve in the best way for us, either by feeling sadness, anger, guilt, or even relief, without shame or judgment. These feelings are all valid and normal in the grieving process. Sharing these feelings with others who understand, like other grieving mothers, can foster a sense of connection and help lessen the burden of isolation.

We also need to recognize that, while our motherly instincts might tell us we could have saved our child, sometimes there was truly nothing more we could have done. Accepting this painful reality is one of the first steps toward moving away from self-blame and toward compassion for ourselves.

Gradually, carrying on becomes possible as we learn to entrust our grief to God and allow Him to help us bear this burden. God has walked this journey and knows our pain. Jesus carried our pain and suffering by dying on a cross on our behalf (Hebrews 12:2).

At ten months old, as soon as Sebastian started walking, it appeared as if he was trying to leave home. He was always escaping; going places, he shouldn't (or I thought he shouldn't, but in his toddler's mind, he had no sense of fear or worry). As Sebastian grew, his instinct to explore and push boundaries became clear, reminding me of the bittersweet truth that, no matter how much we cherish their presence, children are destined to move beyond the safety of home.

The Bible tells us our children are a blessing from the Lord. “Children are a heritage from the Lord, offspring a reward from him” (Psalm 127:3). The Bible further recognizes that there will come a time when our children must become independent and navigate their own paths in life beyond our guidance and protection. Even though we are parents forever, we only have our children for a short period of their lives before they are “released” into the world. (Genesis 2:24). Children may leave home and become independent according to their own circumstances, which may differ from those from our own ideas we had envisioned for them. No matter how they leave our homes, it will always be hard to let them go, even under “normal” conditions, such as college, marriage, military service, or a new job.

My identity as a mother had seemed to be destroyed when Sebastian died. I kept asking myself, “Did I still have any value?” and “What was I going to do with my life now?”

Losing Our Identity

A significant challenge confronting grieving mothers is the risk of losing their sense of identity. After the birth of my children, I felt I had lost my “true” identity, and I had been reduced to being simply a mother. While I worked as a nurse, people told me I was doing a good job. In ministry, people lauded my skills and abilities. But when I was changing the thousandth diaper in the last hour, wiping snotty baby noses and drool with my sweatshirt sleeve forty times a day, I felt no one was telling me “good job” and giving me praise for my accomplishments as a mother. I am fortunate to have an awesome husband supporting me in raising our children, but he didn't change jobs; he did what he always did and returned to work. But at the time, I was left home alone, wondering if this was all there was to life.

But being a mother isn't all there is of me.

I'm a wife, a nurse practitioner, a writer, an aunt, and an artist. I'm a costume designer, a baker, a reader, a runner, a hiker, and a daughter. I've been a school nurse, a Naval officer, a bartender, a camp counselor, a Bible study leader, and a craft queen.

However, making my identity in any of these things will eventually disappoint or fail me, or they will fall short in some way. No matter how much fulfillment I may find in my roles as a wife, nurse practitioner, artist, or any of the other hats I wear, these identities are still temporary and imperfect. Each one, at some point, will leave me feeling incomplete or inadequate because circumstances can change in an instant, as when my identity changed after Sebastian died. The loss of my son shattered the foundation I had built my identity upon, forcing me to confront the reality that even the most cherished and meaningful parts of my life are not immune to pain, loss, and disappointment.

I sometimes struggle with making my son's death a part of my "identity." Yes, my son died, but I am more than my son's suicide. At the same time, I can't live my life wondering if I could have changed his ending. If only I were a better mom, or maybe if I only said something different, Sebastian might be alive today. My meanderings won't change what already happened.

"I can't come home, can I?" Sebastian asked me a few hours before he killed himself.

As his mother, I wanted Sebastian to come home. I wanted to take care of him and make everything better. But the life choices Sebastian had made dictated that he couldn't come home. There were consequences for his behaviors, and I couldn't rescue him and take away his pain, but I could pray for my son and encourage him to hang in there.

"You know you can't, not now." I clutched my cell phone tighter, wanting to say different words to comfort him. "I will see you this weekend. You're going to be OK. You've got this, Sebastian."

"I understand why I can't come home, Mom. I love you."

"I love you too, Big Guy."

That final exchange on the phone with Sebastian has lingered in my heart, a painful reminder that sometimes loving our child cannot bridge the gap created by our children's choices and circumstances. As I sat with the ache of that moment, I found myself reflecting on the journey of motherhood itself and how our identities as mothers are shaped long before our children ever speak their first words.

Even before our child's birth, while they were swirling in our wombs, we earned the right to be called "mother." One can be called a mother without "having" a child, but for argument's sake, once we claim a child as our own, we take on the identity of "Mother." It becomes our life, and in the early life of our child and then children, it often consumes us physically, emotionally, and spiritually. However, as children grow older and no longer cling to their mother, they begin to explore their environment, gaining independence.

Eventually, as they age, they will leave home. It is a natural progression of growing up and attaining adulthood.

Empty Nest Syndrome (ENS) is a term used to describe the sadness, grief, and loneliness that can develop after a child leaves their home under "normal" conditions. It's a time of adjustment, trying to figure out what life will be like now that our child has launched out of the nest. It is a regular part of life.[52]

The potential danger of ENS is when a person, typically a mother, has not planned or is in denial about their child leaving home. A mother's identity, for the last 17-20 plus years, has been invested in another person. They may have forgotten what it is like to be an autonomous individual now that their child or children have left home.

With the premature departure of a child due to death by suicide, this sudden destruction of the nest can cause even more intense grief. In some way, a mother switches her identity to that of a grieving mother who lost a child to suicide.

This type of complex grief can become problematic if we continue to identify as this type of mother or person in the ensuing years. This mindset poses the risk of unconsciously idolizing our deceased children, thereby impeding our progress in the grieving process by causing us to cling to the past. Such an outlook can hinder our development, cause us to lose focus, and divert our attention from other important aspects of life.

---

52 Burns, Jim. *Finding Joy in the Empty Nest: Discover Purpose and Passion in the Next Phase of Life*. Zondervan Books, 2022.

Finding My True Identity

> Therefore, since we are surrounded by such a great cloud of witnesses, let us throw off everything that hinders and the sin that so easily entangles. And let us run with perseverance the race marked out for us, fixing our eyes on Jesus, the pioneer and perfecter of faith. For the joy set before him, he endured the cross, scorning its shame, and sat down at the right hand of the throne of God. Consider him who endured such opposition from sinners, so that you will not grow weary and lose heart (Hebrews 12:1–3).
>
> I need to remember to keep my eyes on Jesus.
>
> Who I am must be rooted in who Jesus is.

After experiencing a devastating loss, remaining rooted in Jesus can be both a challenge and a lifeline. The pain of our messy mourning may threaten to overwhelm our sense of identity. Still, the context above reminds us that our true identity is found in Christ, not solely in our roles as parents or in the circumstances we face.

Remaining rooted in Jesus after loss is a lifelong journey. It requires perseverance, honesty, community, and a willingness to let Him redefine our identity. My greatest longing is to praise God forever. Jesus is the one who died for me, a sinner. He is the one who rescued me and delivered me into a spacious place when the storms of life came and will still come upon me. Jesus is the one who forgives my wrongs and no longer remembers them. He was the one I immediately turned to and who I cried to over and over again in my agonizing grief after my son died. Jesus was the one who knew my pain and suffering because he took them to the cross.

I have come to realize that it is essential to remember that my sense of identity is ultimately found in Jesus, not in my children, whether they are with me or not.

The Greek word ὄγκος, meaning "throw off" or "throw aside," refers to removing any obstacles that might hinder our progress in our lives.[53] "Throwing off" may mean eventually becoming reconciled to the loss of our child. It doesn't imply that we forget them (see Chapter 16), but it may require that, at some point, we consider whether, in our grief, we have forgotten that God absolutely loves us. He sent His son to die for us, offering us life and hope through Him.

We need to think of grief like a marathon. We are not in a quick sprint that is over quickly. We are running to endure, and to do this, we need to set aside things that hold us back from moving forward. I have found this by fixing my eyes on Jesus, who is "the perfector [of my] faith" (Hebrews 12:2). Jesus has set the way for me to follow. I have found that Jesus knows all the bumps, ruts, holes, and cracks that have hindered me from going forward. Jesus removed all my roadblocks by his death and resurrection on the cross. Keeping my eyes focused on Jesus is essential because He set the example of how to endure and persevere, looking beyond all pain and suffering. He knows what lies ahead, which is life eternal with Him. We are assured a "better

---

53 Moo, Douglas J. Hebrews. Zondervan Exegetical Commentary on the New Testament, Zondervan Academic, 2024.

resurrection" (Hebrews 11:35), signifying that one day I will have perfect peace and a healed body once I have left this earthly home.[54]

How will we know if our identity entirely rests on Jesus? "When the thing we are most looking forward to in eternity is praising him forever."[55] By centering our identity in Jesus, we can experience a deep sense of peace that sustains us even as we navigate the pain and confusion in our messy mourning.

---

54 Moo, Douglas J. *Hebrews*. Zondervan Exegetical Commentary on the New Testament, Zondervan Academic, 2024.

55 Keller, Timothy. *Romans 1-7 for You.* The Good Book Company, 2014.

THOUGHTS TO CONSIDER

1. How have you viewed your role or identity during this grieving process?
2. How has your identity shaped how you view your life and grief?
3. Has your grief drawn you closer to God or pushed you away?
4. Who or what are you focusing on right now?
5. How has losing a child to suicide hastened or intensified the Empty Nest Syndrome for you?

CHAPTER 15

We Can't Do It on Our Own

"The Lord himself goes before you and will be with you; he will never leave you nor forsake you. Do not be afraid; do not be discouraged."
—Deuteronomy 31:8

"Scotty, I can't lead this small group anymore."

Three months had passed since Sebastian's death. I had been guiding a small group of six teenage girls for two years, with the intention to continue until their high school graduation. Our weekly gatherings for food, fellowship, Bible study, and life sharing had been such a joy. But after Sebastian's passing, I found myself unable to lead, consumed by the overwhelming grief of losing my son.

I had confided in Scotty, our church youth pastor, my concerns about continuing to lead this group. I wasn't in the best place to lead. I was still a mess, and I was still crying all the time. Hence, instead of giving me the standard pat answer of," It's OK, I totally understand why you can't do this anymore," he instead challenged me with these words,

"You know, Jackie, I still think you should continue meeting with your girls."

I'm pretty sure my eyes bugged out, and I responded with, "But I'm not even reading my Bible anymore. I am not qualified to lead a Bible study. My brain isn't working anymore."

It was then that Scotty offered a perspective I had not considered. He suggested, "I believe it's important for you to continue meeting with them, not for a structured Bible study, but for them to witness how you are navigating this profound loss of Sebastian."

He smiled and repeated, "Allow them to see you grieve and live your life."

Therefore, I did. Not because I wanted to, but because my pastor challenged me to live out my faith amid my painful grief. My girls (as I lovingly called them) saw me cry almost every week. I talked about Sebastian, and we prayed together. We laughed, cried, and ate cheese pizza. I attended their music concerts, sat through numerous other school programs, and then their high school graduations two years later. It was exhausting and rewarding at the same time. We did life together, and I'm glad I listened to Scotty. This experience reaffirmed my belief in the healing power of faith.

After such a devastating loss of a child by suicide, it is "natural" to draw into ourselves and isolate from those who might want to help us. Hodges and Leonard write, "Isolating yourself from other people can seem an easy choice when you are in deep grief, but too much isolation will intensify your pain."[56] It is easy not to respond to texts or messages when you are in such pain. I have written in previous chapters about how I initially avoided people during my grief. I physically, emotionally, and spiritually couldn't, or didn't think I could be with people. They didn't understand what I was going through. They hadn't lost a child to suicide. It is hard to think of others when you are deeply immersed in your own suffering. That's why when Scotty challenged me in my grief, it made me look outside myself to see other people in their grief and suffering as well.

Even in our grief, it's our tendency, at least in American culture, not to appear weak. We want people to think we are doing great when we are not. We don't want to be a burden, but in reality, we are not. We need to admit when we need help, and when we do, it will be amazing how much better we will begin to feel. Admitting one's weakness is essential to experiencing God's help. The apostle Paul was not afraid to write about his shortcomings; throughout his letters in the New Testament, he teaches that acknowledging our own weakness allows God's strength and will to shine through us. He proclaims that God's will is revealed when we admit our weaknesses. "In the same way, the Spirit helps us in our weakness. We do not know what we ought to pray for, but the Spirit himself intercedes for us through wordless groans" (Romans 8:26). We can be encouraged by

56 Hodges, S. J., and Kathy Leonard. Grieving with Hope: Finding Comfort as You Journey Through Loss. Baker Books, 2011.

Paul's words when he wrote, "If I must boast, I will boast of the things that show my weakness" (2 Corinthians 11:30). Paul's letters encourage us and permit us to share our pain and suffering with God.

God gives us the strength to endure.

> "But he [God] said to me, 'My grace is sufficient for you, for my power is made perfect in weakness.' Therefore, I will boast all the more gladly about my weaknesses, so that Christ's power may rest on me. That is why, for Christ's sake, I delight in weaknesses, in insults, in hardships, in persecutions, in difficulties. For when I am weak, then I am strong" (2 Corinthians 12:9–10).

It's important to let others know when we're struggling; otherwise, they may not realize we need support unless we tell them. For example, if you share with a friend that you're feeling overwhelmed, they might offer to listen or help with daily tasks. Being open about our emotions allows those around us to provide the care and understanding we genuinely need. Sharing my pain with others was a crucial step in my healing journey. J.I. Packer once wrote,

> Grace is God drawing us sinners closer and closer to Himself. How does God in grace prosecute this purpose? Not by shielding us from assault by the world, the flesh, and the devil, nor by protecting us from burdensome and frustrating circumstances, nor by shielding us from trouble created by our own temperament and psychology; but rather by exposing us to all these things, so as to overwhelm us with a sense of our own inadequacy, and to drive us to cling to him more closely. This is the ultimate reason, from

> our standpoint, why God fills our lives with troubles and perplexities of one sort and another—it is to ensure that we shall learn to hold him fast.[57]

Early in my messy mourning, I had a season I called "my season of tears." It felt like I cried all the time for the first two years after Sebastian's death. People would see me crying, and I'd say, "I'm in this season of crying." The more I said this, the less I began to worry about what other people thought. People appreciated that I told them where I was in my life. Not every day is perfect. Most days are not.

What Can I Do Even Though I Don't Want to Do Anything

1. **Get Out the Door and Walk Every Day, Rain or Shine.**

I began walking my dog around the block. I got up early before anyone else was awake and would walk for 45-60 minutes a day. A dog has a schedule, regardless of what has happened to us; they are a great motivator to get ourselves out and face the world. I walked every day, rain or shine, or snow, and in the dark. I discovered I had to do this; I needed it, and I still do it to this day.

It was during this time that I started listening to the Bible every day. In my Bible app, my mind was soothed by Nicky Gumble's British accent as he gave a devotional on the day's reading. I listened to the whole Bible every day for seven years.[58] These daily readings provided a source

57 Packer, J. I. *Knowing God*. IVP, 1973.

58 "The Bible with Nicky and Pippa Gumbel." *Alpha*, bible.alpha.org/en/.

of comfort and strength when I didn't think I could get through the morning.

Sometimes, I was distracted, and my mind wandered as I listened to God's word every morning. My thoughts were scattered that first year, but I held on to the truth that God's words were somehow bathing my broken spirit and covering me with his love and protection. I felt like I was being covered by a force field of God's word, protecting me from the lies my broken heart might accidentally believe.

2. Keep a Regular Routine.

During those first months after Sebastian's death, I didn't want to get out of bed. Getting up meant another day without Sebastian. I didn't want to cook or do meal prep. Looking back, I thank God for all the meals and gift cards delivered to our house during the first few months of our grief. A friend of mine who had lost her son to cancer once told me that I must keep moving and keep a routine. Her words stuck with me. And even though I didn't want to do anything, I started keeping a routine. There is that old saying, "Fake it until you make it." I joined an online exercise group for eighty days. Five days a week for thirty to forty minutes. I did this group three times. It kept me accountable not to stress-eat (which was and can still be my go-to "therapy" when I'm stressed or feeling out of control).

Going to church was difficult, as I had mentioned in previous chapters, but I knew I had to go; it was as if God was compelling me to spend time with Him and other Christians. As I mentioned earlier, I'd attend the earliest service, which was attended by only older congregants who didn't know me. It was easy to slip into the dark sanctuary, hide on the side where I'd cry the whole time, and then I'd slip out once the last song started. The important thing was being in fellowship. It's all about taking baby steps. Eventually, we'll be able to walk, but always with a limp; however, as we move forward, it becomes less noticeable.

3. Find Your Safe People.

I can't stress this enough: we need people to help us in this grief journey, whether we like it or not, and it's not in the best interest of our grieving family if we only utilize them for meeting all our needs when they need us to meet their needs.

Before this horrible thing happened to us, we already had safe people in place that we met with regularly. As I mentioned previously, I had a few ladies who became my fortress, mostly by their mere presence in my house, and this helped me bear this horrible burden.

My husband and I had attended a church small group before Sebastian died. They, too, prayed and encouraged us as we were struggling with our son's addictions and rehab. However, after Sebastian's death, I was no longer able to attend this group. Steve continued to go, and the ladies would send me texts and messages of encouragement, but I was unable to return them. I couldn't do it. I didn't want their pity, even though they weren't offering that. They only wanted to help me in my grief. Sometimes, we don't go back, and that can be appropriate as well.

It's essential to permit ourselves not to attend events or gatherings that make us uncomfortable, especially in the days of early grief. There is no shame in stepping back when needed. At the same time, for those of us who follow

Jesus, faith sometimes prompts us to step into places that stretch us or feel uncomfortable. God can use our grief in ways we never expected, working through our struggles to bring about growth and healing.

I experienced this firsthand when I was challenged to continue leading my girls' group. Even though it was frankly awful for a long time. Every week, gathering with the group felt overwhelming, and there were moments when I wondered if I could keep going. Yet, persevering through those hard seasons taught me invaluable lessons about resilience and the importance of community. Over time, the girls' group became more than an obligatory commitment; it transformed us into a place of shared support and genuine connection.

Recently, I had lunch with a couple of my girls. We began talking about our meetings after Sebastian's death. One said, "Even in your pain, you were still there for us. You were consistent, and you never abandoned us. We will never forget how you continued to meet with us."

Even in our brokenness, coming together can offer comfort, encouragement, and a reminder that we aren't alone.

Faith often leads us into uncomfortable spaces, not to make us suffer, but to help us grow. By trusting God and allowing ourselves to be vulnerable in these moments, we open ourselves to unexpected healing and growth. My own journey with the girls' group revealed to me that God can bring light into the darkest places, using our pain to foster deeper relationships and offer renewed hope to others. Seeing my pain allowed them to share their hurts as well.

Eventually, we all need to venture back into the world. Grief may make us feel isolated, but we aren't meant to navigate it alone. Stepping forward, even with a limp, is an act of courage and faith. Over time, the support and compassion we find in the community can help us heal.

4. The Importance of Grief Groups.

Mothers who have lost a child to suicide experience the same challenges that other mothers face after losing a child to different types of death; grief, sadness, anger, and disbelief are universal emotions experienced after any loss. Suicidal grief is unique as it can also manifest emotions of shame, guilt, self-blame, and rejection. "The effects of sigma and trauma may further complicate these painful experiences."[59] Because of these additional emotions, those who have lost a child to suicide are less likely to attend a support group. One way we can help those affected by suicide who are not ready to participate in a support group is to offer to go with them and be an advocate.

Suicide survivor support groups can be beneficial because they provide a safe space to share our stories and not feel like we are being judged. Everyone in the group has lost someone they love to suicide; they know how we feel. They understand the thoughts, the triggers, the stigmas, and the irrational guilt feelings. Additionally, Young et al. states,

59 Young, Ilanit Tal, Amanda Iglewicz, Deanna Glorioso, and Sidney Zisook. "Suicide Bereavement and Complicated Grief." *Dialogues in Clinical Neuroscience*, vol. 14, no. 2, 2012, pp. 177–186, doi:10.31887/DCNS.2012.14.2/iyoung.

The bonds that develop among people can be powerful as they join a club whose "dues" are high and as they offer each other mutual support. Through such supports, individuals may receive helpful suggestions for taking care of real-life obligations such as dealing with estates and legal issues: talking to others, including children; developing fitting memorials for the deceased; coping with holidays and special events; and setting realistic goals for one's new life, which now has such a vast and unfilled void.

GriefShare is a 13-week support group designed to help individuals navigate the grief process. As a GriefShare leader, I have witnessed those who have lost loved ones discover and gain more understanding about the difficult and complex emotions that come with any loss. Though it is not specifically geared to those who have lost a child to suicide, the weekly videos do interview families who have lost loved ones to suicide. GriefShare provides a safe place to "learn helpful ways of coping with grief, in all its unpredictability, and gain solid support each step of the way."[60]

5. The Role of Individual Counseling.

Individual counselors, therapists, biblical counselors, and church counselors can all play an essential role in helping a mother process her grief and loss of her child.

As mentioned previously, I sought out a grief therapist after the first anniversary of my son's death. I felt adrift, and for the first time in my life, I had no purpose. It seemed like everyone around was doing great (or I thought to

---

60 "GriefShare: Grief Recovery Support Groups." GriefShare, griefshare.org.

myself), my husband's new company was thriving, and this kept him "busy." My daughter was recently married and was planning her next move (to New Zealand!). I felt like I had nothing in me anymore. It was then that I started writing about Sebastian. Writing helped me process my grief in ways I didn't imagine could happen. I would write anything that came to mind, bring it to my therapist, and, as part of our session, read my words aloud. It was reading these sentences aloud that made what happened to me a reality. Needless to say, I'd start to cry and would develop a headache by the end of each session. Still, over the nine months we met, I was able to start letting go of the pain and anger I had towards Sebastian; then the real healing began.

Each session forced me to confront feelings I had tried to ignore: sadness, confusion, guilt, and even resentment. The therapy sessions didn't take my pain away. Still, it softened it, helping me realize my scattered emotions were common and I wasn't as alone as I thought. As the weeks turned into months, I noticed small shifts in myself: I laughed again, I slept a little better, and I found comfort in remembering the good memories with Sebastian instead of only focusing on the tragedy of his death. Letting go of my anger didn't mean forgetting or excusing what happened; it meant freeing myself to grieve more healthily and to begin rebuilding hope. Through this process, I learned that healing can't be completed in a short period of time. Still, it is possible to move forward when we allow ourselves to be vulnerable and accept support from others who truly understand.

Remember that your messy mourning is uniquely your own, and there's no "right" way to heal. The pain you feel is a testament to the love you have for your child, and it's acceptable to let yourself experience every emotion: sadness, anger, confusion, and even moments of hope. Healing is not about forgetting your child, but about allowing yourself to rediscover beauty and meaning in your life once again. Surround yourself with people who understand, seek support when you're ready, and know that asking for help is a sign of strength, not weakness.

I encourage you to take gentle steps forward, even when it feels uncomfortable. Each small act, from sharing your story to joining a group, writing your feelings, or simply allowing yourself to laugh again, is a victory. You're not alone, and by opening your heart to what God has made available, you create space for both healing and hope to grow.

THOUGHTS TO CONSIDER

1. Have you thought about joining a support group for suicide survivors? If not, why?
2. What actions do you take to maintain your well-being daily? Create a list of activities that can help you take care of yourself.
3. Have you observed any changes in your daily routine following the loss of your child? What adjustments could help you return to a regular routine?
4. Counseling can be beneficial for anyone who has lost a child. What steps, if any, have you taken to schedule an initial visit to a counselor? Have friends or family made recommendations?

CHAPTER 16

Death Is Not the Last Goodbye

"Do not let your hearts be troubled. You believe in God; believe also in me. My Father's house has many rooms; if that were not so, would I have told you that I am going there to prepare a place for you? And if I go and prepare a place for you, I will come back and take you to be with me that you also may be where I am. You know the way to the place where I am going."
John 14:1–4

Six months after Sebastian's passing, I embarked on my first solo flight to Chicago for a pediatric nurse practitioner conference. The mix of nerves and excitement was palpable as I anticipated reuniting with my fellow University of Washington alums. Some of them had attended Sebastian's funeral, but this was the first time I'd be away from my husband and daughter. I was still navigating the early stages of my grief, and tears would often well up in the most unexpected situations. I couldn't control them. People didn't know what to say when I began to cry, and I always felt I had to explain what had happened. It became exhausting after a while.

When the flight attendants announced my boarding zone, I joined my fellow passengers who were waiting to scan their tickets. Once aboard the aircraft, I wended my way down the passageway and found my window seat on the left side. After placing my carry-on item in the overhead bin, I scooted around the fellow passengers already sitting in our row's aisle and middle seat.

Then, without warning, a panic attack seized me. My body began to tremble, my breath caught in my throat, and tears welled up in my eyes.

This unexpected thought began to race through my brain: I had to find my phone and tell Steve and Isabel that I loved them. I knew my thoughts were irrational, but I had to do this before the plane left the runway.

What if the plane crashed and Steve and Isabel didn't hear me say I loved them?

I couldn't remember if I told them I loved them. They had to know.

My last dying words had to be, "I love you."

While leaning down to search for my phone in one of the numerous pockets of my backpack, I heard the flight attendant begin the usual departure announcements. Grabbing my phone, I could see out of the corner of my eye a smiling flight attendant wearing her orange-blow-up life vest. A chirpy voice overhead announced, "In the unlikely event of an emergency...." I started panting, trying to will away the imminent panic attack precisely as the same happy disembodied voice announced, "In the case of a sudden loss of oxygen pressure in the cabin...." I fumbled through the message thread, searching for a previous text that contained both names.

The plane taxied towards the runway when the flight attendant announced, "All passengers must put their cell phones in Airplane Mode." I frantically texted Steve and Isabel,

"I love you both. I'm taking off."

Sucking in air through my nostrils, I waited, my breathing still erratic and my palms sweating profusely. I couldn't turn the phone off—not yet. I had to know they got the message.

They had to read my message before takeoff.

The aircraft picked up speed and ascended over Portland, and I watched as the Columbia River disappeared from my view.

Then it happened. My phone vibrated, and I looked at my screen.

"Love you, Mama!!"

"Love you, Sweetheart! (with a pink tulip emoji)," from Steve."

Instantly, my breathing relaxed, my heart slowed to a normal rate, and my hands were no longer sweaty. I turned off Airplane Mode, closed my eyes, and thanked God for allowing me to share my love with my family.

Ever since that flight to Chicago, whenever a family member traveled by plane, it became an obsession for me to tell Steve and Isabel I loved them. I needed them to know that if I died on that plane, or if they died, my last words to them were of love and affection, not of arguments, misunderstandings, or stupid quarrels.

Two significant events, separated by forty years, may have contributed to my reaction on the plane. The first event occurred when I was eighteen, during my first year of college. My mother died suddenly of a stroke. The month prior, we had argued while I was home over Christmas break. I was extremely angry with her, so I didn't say goodbye when I returned to college. We were still not speaking to each other when I received the word of her death; I didn't tell her I loved her.

The day before Sebastian died, I did tell him that I loved him. I had hung up the phone, not realizing that in less than twelve hours, a police chaplain would be knocking at our front door, telling us he had died.

Both these experiences shaped my desire to always express my love to my surviving family members before parting ways. Still, somehow it intensified after I lost my son.

After eight years, this ritual of saying "I love you" transformed from a source of anxiety into a meaningful tradition. The weight of my grief has finally lifted, and I no longer panic before a flight. Once, I forgot to text Isabel when Steve and I were traveling to Europe, and I didn't panic (Steve told me later he had texted Isabel for us).

The reality is that I have no control over the future; only God does. In the same way, I couldn't control what happened to my son or mother, I have no control over the pilots, drivers, or train conductors who carry my family or me to our scheduled or unscheduled destinations. My magic words of "I love you" will not change any outcomes for the future; these three words are not a spell or some magical incantation to protect us from evil, but to a certain extent, the phrase "I love you" is an acknowledgment of the affirmation and affection we have for each other in our family.

Healing can come in unexpected ways in these moments if we look for it and allow it to happen.

Death does not need to be the last goodbye.

I believe that death is only the last step we will all take before we are finally set free from all the grief, suffering, and pain we have endured our entire lives.

Early in my grief, I would think and say things like, "I can't wait to see Sebastian again." My husband longed for heaven because he felt he couldn't bear this pain on earth and wanted to be reunited with our son. I would tell my friends, "I was going to push Jesus aside and see my son." I had lost sight of Jesus, the healer of all my pain. Over time, my thoughts have shifted back to Jesus, who is the source of my hope for salvation.

On the final day of my life on this planet, and after I have taken my last breath, I will finally see Jesus in all his glory. Sebastian and all my friends and family who have placed their trust in Jesus will be there to greet me. Because in the end, all that matters is Jesus.

Jesus once told his followers, "Do not let your hearts be troubled" (John 14:1). God has a special place waiting for us after we leave this earthly home. Jesus went on to say, "My Father's house has many rooms; if that were not so, would I have told you that I am going there to prepare a place for you" (John 14:2). These words offered profound reassurance to his disciples, especially during times of uncertainty and loss. Knowing that Jesus acknowledged their fears and anxieties and responded with a promise of peace and eternal belonging would have been incredibly comforting. His assurance that God had prepared a place for them meant that, despite the hardships and grief they faced, there was hope beyond this life, a future in God's presence where all suffering would be replaced by peace and rest.

For those struggling with grief, such words from Jesus invite trust and the promise of healing. These promises are not only for the future, but also for now. They serve as reminders that, even in the midst of our messy mourning, we are never truly alone. Jesus' words encouraged his followers to take their eyes off the waves and storms of fear and pain, and shift their focus to Jesus, who offers us hope.

I know by faith that Sebastian has his place in heaven with Jesus. God promises us that he will remain faithful and true. We can always rely on Him. God said that He would never leave us, nor would He ever turn His back on us (Deuteronomy 31:6). He loved us so much that He showed this love by allowing His Son, Jesus, to die in our place, so that we might live with Him forever. God has a place for us with Him. He says He has many rooms. A space is guaranteed upon request. We only have to ask Jesus.

THOUGHTS TO CONSIDER

1. What are your thoughts about heaven? Have they changed since the loss of your child? Why or why not?
2. Many people wonder about their loved ones in heaven, and that's natural. Knowing our children are healed can be comforting; they are at peace. Does this comfort you? Why or why not?
3. I often felt guilty when I would think about my son in heaven, instead of Jesus. Do you think Jesus cares about this? Why or why not?
4. Were you able to tell your child you loved them before they died? If not, how did that affect you, and has your perspective changed over time?
5. Have you experienced a panic attack following the loss of your child? If so, what memory or sensation triggered it, and what do you believe contributed to this response? What strategies are you employing to support yourself during these occurrences?

CHAPTER 17

Building Our Ebenezers: Letting Go and Never Forgetting

"Brothers and sisters, I do not consider myself yet to have taken hold of it. But one thing I do: Forgetting what is behind and straining toward what is ahead."
—Philippians 3:13

Dinner was tense, with long silences and worried glances exchanged as our dear friends described their child's latest setbacks—the missed calls, the desperate late-night texts, the constant uncertainty about what to-morrow might bring. Their voices trembled as they recounted sleepless nights and the overwhelming fear of what could happen next. As we listened to their story, memories of our own difficult times resurfaced: the late-night anxiety, the ache of helplessness, and the heartbreak of watching a beloved child struggle. We understood their pain and offered empathy. Steve asked if we could pray for them, not just as friends, but as fellow travelers on a similar, painful road.

After the meal was over and the four of us were sharing a piece of pie, our friends apologized and said,

> "Our problems are not nearly as bad as yours. Your son is dead. We feel awful for telling you our problems."

We reassured them we were doing well and that we wanted to listen to their concerns and be there for them.

Afterward, on the drive home, Steve said,

> "Honestly, I am doing good. Do you think I should feel guilty that I'm in a better place?"

> "No," I said, "We don't have to worry about Sebastian anymore. He is in a better place, and we *are* doing well."

Absolutely, we missed Sebastian, but somehow, without realizing it, our grief had softened and had become more manageable. It didn't consume us like it once had. Some days, I'd forgotten how awful I once felt. It was our faith in God that sustained us, reminding us that Sebastian was in a better place and that we were doing better.

I distinctly remember those earlier days before Sebastian's death; I was always anxious, wondering if Sebastian was "safe" and whether he was still alive. Whenever I went a few days without hearing from him, a sick feeling would settle deep in my stomach, quickly turning into painful aches and pounding headaches. The pain in my stomach was a constant, dull throb that made it nearly impossible to focus on anything else, and the headaches often left me feeling drained and unable to cope with even the simplest tasks.

Steve and I had many discussions and arguments about the best way to "handle" Sebastian's ongoing addictions and mental health issues. We spent numerous hours in counseling, as a couple, trying to come up with a mutual game plan for dealing with Sebastian's "problems." As a couple, we examined Sebastian's struggles and difficulties from two distinct family backgrounds. I tended to be more merciful with Sebastian, and Steve was stricter. We both loved our son dearly, but we viewed his struggles from different perspectives, which caused tension in our relationships with each other and with Sebastian. I was "the weak link," meaning I tended to give in whenever Sebastian needed or wanted something. Sebastian knew this and would, at times, try to use it against his father's better judgment.

We needed help with Sebastian, and we had to build a united front.

Our therapist played a crucial role in our healing journey. He listened, offered advice, and helped us develop tools and a better game plan as a couple. About five years later, we began to realize that we were gradually finding ourselves in a better place, and we were indeed moving forward in our grief, sometimes without even realizing it. This gradual healing process is a continual testament to the power of God and the support of family and friends.

The Bible tells us that King David reached a similar point in his grief.

King David had an extramarital affair with Bathsheba, the wife of Uriah the Hittite (2 Samuel 11:1–24). Upon learning that Bathsheba had become pregnant with his child, David attempted to conceal the affair by having Uriah intentionally killed in a battle. After the designated period of time of mourning, David married Bathsheba.

What David did was displeasing to God.

The prophet Nathan confronted David with a parable, revealing his sin and pronouncing God's judgment upon him. Nathan declared that while God had forgiven David, the child Bathsheba bore would die as a consequence of his sin.

Subsequently, after the child was born, he fell gravely ill. David prayed and fasted for seven nights while lying prostrate on the ground, that God would spare his innocent baby.

It wasn't the baby's fault that David had sinned.

Despite David's fasting and prayers, his baby died, fulfilling the prophecy God had given to Nathan.

No one wanted to tell David that his child had died, but he soon realized what had happened. David got up off the ground, took a shower, and went into the House of God to worship. Afterward, he went home and ate a meal. His attendants were shocked by David's apparent lack of concern for his dead child. The story continues in 2 Samuel 12:21–22:

> His attendants asked him, "Why are you acting this way? While the child was alive, you fasted and wept, but now that the child is dead, you get up and eat!"

> He answered, "While the child was still alive, I fasted and wept. I thought, 'Who knows? The Lord may be gracious to me and let the child live.' But now that he is dead, why should I go on fasting? Can I bring him back again? I will go to him, but he will not return to me."

Like David, I had also prayed for years for Sebastian's healing. I prayed for his mental health issues, his poor choices, and his mistakes, especially those that made me mad, upset, or left me at a loss for words. I often didn't know what to do anymore. These prayers became a constant companion, shaping how I saw Sebastian and myself, and testing the limits of my faith.

There came a time when I realized Sebastian taking his life might, in reality, happen, and I might not be able to stop it. I didn't want this to happen, but I somehow knew that this might be my reality unless something miraculous happened. I continued to pray for a miracle and that God would somehow intervene in my son's life. I refused to give up hope.

When Sebastian died, I was devastated, but at the same time, I knew in my heart that Sebastian was no longer in pain and suffering. I was still suffering, but Sebastian was finally safe and at peace. God had healed him. Like David, I couldn't bring Sebastian back, and I wouldn't want him back as he was while he was alive.

David's story resonates profoundly with my own experience. After David lost his son, he recognized he was never in control; he could neither undo the past nor save his child. David's grief was terrible, but upon accepting his son's death, he found the strength to rise, worship, and carry on, trusting in God's wisdom and mercy. Similarly, when Sebastian passed, a part of me wanted desperately to change the outcome, to somehow reverse time and bring him back. However, I came to realize, comparably as David did, that my prayers, though constant and heartfelt, could not alter the reality of Sebastian's suffering or his choice. What I could do was entrust Sebastian to God's care, knowing he was finally healed by God and at peace, beyond all earthly pain.

The story of David reminds us that grief and loss are not signs of weak faith but are more or less moments that can shape our trust in God. David's response, which seemed strange to his servants, to worship God, accept what had happened, and hope that he'd see his son again, encourages me to continue the messy mourning I am walking through now. I hold onto the same faith that comforted David, knowing that Sebastian and David's son are in God's loving arms, free from the struggles that marked their brief lives here.

Like David, I cannot bring my son back. Since Sebastian's death, a peace has developed in my heart that I can't explain, but I know it could only have come from God. This faith in God's healing power has been a significant source of comfort and strength. "And the peace of God, which transcends all understanding, will guard your hearts and your minds in Christ Jesus" (Philippians 4:7). I look forward to the day when I get to see Sebastian again, healed and at peace.

Building Our Ebenezers

"Then Samuel took a stone and set it up between Mizpah and Shen.

He named it Ebenezer, saying, "Thus far the Lord has helped us."

1 Samuel 7:12

Just as biblical stories recount the gathering of stones to remember God's faithfulness, Sebastian had his own way of collecting reminders from our journeys together. Sebastian's love for rocks was a joy to behold; he would eagerly collect them wherever we went. On our road trips, stopping at a rest area would inevitably lead to Sebastian and his sister scampering around the mounds of dirt and returning with handfuls of rocks that would ultimately end up on the car floor.

Sebastian had boxes of rocks, each with its own story. He was particularly fond of geodes, often hammering them apart on the sidewalk with a gleeful smile.

Without fail, on our annual road trip to New Mexico to see Steve's parents, when we reached the outer edge of Moab, Utah, Sebastian would yell, "Can we stop at the Rock Shop?"

The Moab Rock Shop is a rock hunter's paradise. It has everything for both current and future geologists and paleontologists. You can rummage through the store and find everything from fossils and dinosaur bones and teeth to arrowheads, polished rocks, rock jewelry, and many other unique items. We always stopped, and I'd have to set a limit on the number of stones the kids could purchase.

It was after Sebastian died that I rediscovered his hoard of hundreds of rocks, weighing hundreds of pounds, which appeared to be stored in numerous boxes in his bedroom, on his shelves, in the attic, and under his bed. I was at a loss as to what to do with them.

The Bible recounts numerous stories of God commanding His people to gather stones and pile them up as reminders of His power and as a sign of His blessings upon those who obey His commands.

After leading the people of Israel across the Jordan River to claim the land promised to Moses, Joshua, instructed by God, collected twelve stones (one from each tribe of Israel) from the river's center. These stones were to be used in constructing an altar as a permanent reminder of God's provision, divine aid, and assistance for the people of Israel as they entered the Promised Land (Joshua 4:1–9).

When God helped the Israelites defeat the Philistines, Samuel, the last judge of Israel, took a stone and placed it at the site where the Israelites had won the battle between the cities of Mizpah and Shiloh. He called this stone "Ebenezer, saying, 'Thus far has the Lord helped us'" (1 Samuel 7:12). The word "Ebenezer" comes from the Hebrew phrase "stone of help."[61]

A few months after Sebastian's death, when I finally had the courage to clean out his room, I collected all his rocks and placed them in clear glass jars of different sizes. I then put them on display in various locations around the house. No one coming into the house would suspect they were Sebastian's rocks unless I mentioned it to them.

I couldn't get rid of Sebastian's rocks.

---

61 "Ebenezer." *NIV Exhaustive Concordance Dictionary.* Zondervan. 2015.

Over the last eight years, these rocks have become my Ebenezers; they remind me of all the wonderful things God has done for me during this time.

My Ebenezers help me remember that God does not forget his promises. He has been faithful to carry me through these years of grief. God has been with me the whole time, and even though at times I did not "feel" His presence, He was still with me in my darkest place, guiding me through the darkness into His light. I'm thankful for His love and mercy in my life.

My Ebenezers remind me every day of Sebastian; I will never forget him.

My Ebenezers remind me not to forget my blessings. It is easy to overlook our blessings during times of pain and suffering. When I wonder where God is and why He lets things happen, I will remember what He did for me in my pain and suffering. He never promised to keep me from hard things. Still, he always promised he would never leave me nor forsake me: "Be strong and courageous. Do not be afraid or terrified because of them, for the Lord your God goes with you; he will never leave you nor forsake you" (Deuteronomy 31:6, Hebrews 13:5).

Ebenezer Blessings

- I'm thankful for the twenty-three years I had Sebastian on this earth.
- I'm thankful that Sebastian is healed and whole with Jesus.

- I'm thankful that my marriage to Steve has remained strong despite our tragedy. We know we couldn't have done this without God's help.
- I'm thankful for my relationship with my daughter, Isabel, and her husband, Brennan.
- I'm thankful for my friends who have supported me in my grief and suffering, coming alongside me and bearing my burdens.
- Finally, I'm thankful that my Ebenezers gives me the strength and conviction to tell others about all the good things God has done and continues to do in my life.

THOUGHTS TO CONSIDER

1. What does the term "Ebenezer" mean to you in the context of this chapter, and how can it serve as a reminder during difficult times?
2. What role do relationships—such as those with family, friends, and God—play in handling grief and maintaining hope as described in this chapter?
3. How can identifying and reflecting on one's own "Ebenezers" contribute to healing and finding purpose after a significant loss?
4. What are your "Ebenezers" and how can they help remind you of the good things God has done for you after the loss of your child?
5. In what ways does the author find strength in their faith despite the tragedy of losing her son? How can this help you?

CHAPTER 18

Grieving with Hope

Something quite unexpected has happened. It came this morning early. For various reasons, not in themselves at all mysterious, my heart was lighter than it had been for many weeks.[62]
—C.S. Lewis

It had been six years, but the long line of evergreens, standing as somber sentinels on both sides of the road, looked strangely familiar as we drove past them in the Oregon darkness. It was early March, and the freezing fog that swirled gracefully in and around their ghostly trunks and limbs gave them an eerie façade. At the same time, the manufactured piles of snow, higher than our car, plowed

62 Lewis, C. S. *A Grief Observed*. HarperOne, 2015.

earlier in the day, which blocked our peripheral view and made us feel as if we were driving through a dark twenty-mile tunnel, provided us with a safe passage through Mount Hood National Forest on our two-day road trip to Arizona.

"I had forgotten about the trees." I looked over to Steve, who nodded in agreement. He had been navigating our next stop from the passenger seat with his phone.

The last time we drove through this stretch of deserted, wooded highway towards the high-desert town of Madras, we were on our monthly visit to Sebastian in Bend. On that hot, sunny day, thousands of other drivers were heading in the opposite direction, leaving this area after experiencing the best viewing of a total solar eclipse in the world in August 2017. For a short period, Madras's population of 6,000 swelled to about 100,000 as sun chasers, naturalists, hippies, and other adventure lovers descended upon this small town to experience the "path of totality" as the sun disappeared behind the moon for approximately two minutes. The United States hadn't seen anything like this since its founding in 1776.

We spent the last weekend visiting Sebastian, discussing the eclipse he had experienced at the epicenter of the world at that time. He seemed to be doing well in rehab. And then he wasn't.

Sebastian died twenty days later.

We hadn't been back to Bend ever since.

According to Google Maps' directions, the drive from our current location to Isabel and Brennan's home outside of Phoenix would take approximately twenty-one hours, covering 1,300 miles through Oregon, Nevada, and Arizona.

However, as I took note of the towns the app had us driving through, I quickly noticed that we would have to pass by Bend, Oregon. I wasn't sure I could make that drive; therefore, I looked for alternative routes to Arizona, trying to avoid that part of Oregon. California was an option, but storms and flooding were occurring there, which meant we would have to drive through hazardous conditions.

There was no way I could go to Bend. I avoided Bend on all social media. I blocked my friend's photos, the ones they shared of their stunning images of Smith Rock, the epicenter of Sebastian's death by suicide.

"Maybe it's time to take baby steps, my love." My husband told me as I lamented about where our trip would take us.

"I don't know Steve. I told myself I'd never go back. I don't know if I'm ready."

"What if we leave Friday night after work?" Steve suggested. "That way we won't have to see anything because of the darkness."

We settled on a drive that took us to Prineville, Oregon, and there we would spend the night. It was forty miles away from Bend, and we could avoid seeing that area in the daylight. Hopefully, we wouldn't see anything resembling Smith Rock.

But even the darkness couldn't stop me from remembering what had happened.

"Steve, the sign says 30 miles to Bend. Did we miss a turn? We can't go to Bend!" We had gotten through the snow-covered mountain, and we were driving in pitch blackness, with only passing cars lighting our way. I could see the direction of the windy road by the occasional flickers of light from the headlights of approaching vehicles in the distance. Overhead, billions of stars twinkled through our sunroof.

Steve looked up from the GPS. "We're not going to Bend. We're on the right road."

"Are you sure?" The clock on the dashboard read 10:30, and the temperature read 21 degrees. My nose was running and felt cold, my hands clenched the heated steering wheel, and my heartbeat sped up. "The sign only said Bend, not Prineville."

Steve placed his warm hand on my thigh and gave it a gentle squeeze. "We won't go to Bend. I promise."

Twenty minutes later, we came to a fork in the road. The sign read "Bend" with an arrow pointing left. The arrow pointing right had "Prineville" above it.

As I turned towards the right, away from the town that had produced numerous nightmares over the last five years, a wave of relief washed over me. It was as if a heavy burden had been lifted off my shoulders, and I could finally breathe again. Immediately, I felt a sense of peace wash over me. My shoulders relaxed, my grip on the steering wheel loosened, and my mood lightened. It was a peace that had always been there, but in my anxiety and panic, I had forgotten.

It was a moment of realization for me that I had taken my eyes off Jesus, just as Peter had when he was struggling in the water. In that moment, I understood the power of faith and the importance of keeping my focus on Him, especially in times of distress. Just as I do, the disciples of Jesus also faced moments when their faith was tested, and their attention shifted from Jesus to the surrounding chaos. Their experiences remind us that even those closest to Jesus struggled with doubt and fear.

The disciples of Jesus had had a long day. They were finally packing up what amounted to twelve basketfuls of broken bread, leftovers from when Jesus had performed a miracle and fed over five thousand people in a remote area near the Sea of Galilee (Matthew 14:13–21). After sending the crowd home, instead of resting, Jesus told his disciples to get into a boat and cross to the other side of the sea. He'd meet them later after he went up the mountainside to pray.

While the disciples were in the middle of the lake, a storm developed, and intense winds drove the boat into large waves. The Bible says that Jesus walked out onto the water to meet them. But when the disciples saw Jesus, they were terrified and thought it was a ghost. Jesus told them who he was and not to be afraid. Peter said, "Lord, if it's you... tell me to come to you on the water." Jesus replied, "Come" (Matthew 14:28–29). Peter got out of the boat and began walking towards Jesus. How exciting that must have been initially for Peter. Like Peter, Jesus calls us to Himself, and he asks us to get out of our boat of grief. Similarly, as Peter stepped out of his boat onto the stormy sea, trusting Jesus to help him in the storm, we too are invited to leave our grief and sorrow that has kept us anchored to the shore. Stepping out of the boat requires courage and faith. It means risking vulnerability and daring to believe that Jesus will meet us on the water, even when everything feels uncertain and the storms of grief rage around us.

In the same way, Jesus, who did not abandon Peter when he was sinking, will not leave us struggling alone in our grief. When we answer Jesus' invitation to step out on the water, He gives us the strength to walk through any storm, because He reaches out and grabs us whenever our hearts begin to sink. He promises us peace that surpasses all understanding (Philippians 4:7). By trusting Jesus, we can leave our boat of grief behind and journey towards healing and hope.

One of my favorite psalms, the one I return to again and again, reminds me of God's love for me and how He assures me that no matter how dire my circumstances may be, He will pull me through because He cares for me.

> In my distress I called to the Lord;
> I cried to my God for help.
> From his temple, he heard my voice;
> my cry came before him, into his ears.
>
> He shot his arrows and scattered the enemy,
> with great bolts of lightning he routed them.
> The valleys of the sea were exposed
> and the foundations of the earth laid bare
> at your rebuke, Lord,
> at the blast of breath from your nostrils.
>
> He reached down from on high and took hold of me;
> he drew me out of deep waters.

He rescued me from my powerful enemy,
from my foes, who were too strong for me.
They confronted me in the day of my disaster,
but the Lord was my support.
He brought me out into a spacious place;
he rescued me because he **delighted in me** (Psalm 18:6, 14–19; emphasis added).

God continues to rescue me because he delights in me. Jesus has been with me these entire eight years, including that dreaded drive. Like Peter, even though I knew Jesus and knew He'd care for me, I took my eyes off Him and instead focused on the storms of the past, and began to worry once again. I couldn't see Jesus in the darkness, but He saw me and rescued me. Jesus is Lord over our dark places, and even when we can't see Him, He's there with us, guiding us to take baby steps toward healing and wholeness.

How To Stand Firm in the Storm

I know I could not have gotten through the loss of my son without Jesus.

When life is going well, we believe in and rely on our own confidence and skills. We are the ones who got us to where we are today. This belief often shapes our decisions and fuels our ambition, reminding us that our achievements are a direct result of our perseverance and determination. For instance, after landing a new job or achieving a personal goal, it's natural to attribute our success to our hard work and determination. These accomplishments reinforce our sense of self-reliance and discourage us from seeking help from others. For those who are followers of Jesus, when life is going well, it's easy to set aside time with Jesus and go on with our daily lives. We often unconsciously think to ourselves, "We don't need God."

Then something horrible happens, and we automatically turn to God, and then wonder why God let this awful thing happen to us in the first place. God, therefore, can't be good; A good God wouldn't allow bad things to happen. Our grief becomes self-centered, as grief often does, when we find ourselves turning inward and focusing primarily on our own pain and sorrow.

Before life's challenges arise, whether it's the loss of a child, the stress of unexpected changes, or the weight of everyday struggles, it's essential to build a regular fellowship with God. By spending time in prayer, reading scripture, and seeking God's presence daily, we will establish a solid foundation that helps us stand firm when storms come. For example, during my own journey through grief after losing my son, I discovered that the moments I had spent drawing close to God beforehand gave me strength and comfort when I needed it most. Regular fellowship with God isn't simply a preparation for difficult times; it's what carries us through them, reminding us that we are never alone and that God is always within reach.

As long as we live on this earth, there will always be storms. There are no guarantees that the roof won't come off, the windows won't blow out, or the pipes won't burst; bad things will happen. But if our foundation is firm, through it all, we will remain standing because of the hope that is in us. I'm encouraged by Peter's words when he said to Jesus, "Lord, to whom shall we go? You have the words of eternal life. We have come to believe and to know that you are the Holy One of God" (John 6:68–69).

Even when we are uncertain or struggle with unbelief, God meets us exactly where we are. There are times in life when, despite our best efforts and persistent attempts to solve our problems, we reach a point of desperation.

This is illustrated in the New Testament story of a man bringing his son to Jesus after all other attempts to cure him of an evil spirit had failed.

In his desperation, the man pleaded with Jesus:

Jesus showed concern for this father by asking pertinent questions relating to his son's condition. The father readily answered all of Jesus' questions and then asked him to help his son.

> "'...But if you can do anything, take pity on us and help us.'
> 'If you can?' said Jesus. 'Everything is possible for one who believes.'
> Immediately, the boy's father exclaimed, 'I do believe; help me overcome my unbelief'" (Mark 9:21–24)!

God is present with us even in our doubts and fears. When we struggle to hold onto faith, we can ask for help, trusting that God will sustain us. He gives us the strength to stand firm, and therefore, we can find hope, even in our darkest moments.

This chapter reminds us that life's storms are inevitable, but we are not left to face them alone. By building a steady relationship with God through prayer, scripture, and worship, we can establish a firm foundation that will help us endure even the most severe tragedies. My prayers have changed over the years since Sebastian's death. I have developed a deeper understanding of God's eternal perspective and that this earth is not my forever home. Our journey through grief and hardship can shift from self-centered sorrow to a path of hope and healing when we keep our eyes on Jesus, trusting in his presence and guidance.

THOUGHTS TO CONSIDER

1. What do you think it means to have a "foundation to stand on" during life's storms? How can this foundation be built and maintained?
2. In what ways does grief become self-centered, and how can we shift our focus during challenging times to find hope and healing?
3. How can the idea of boasting in weakness, as mentioned by Paul in 2 Corinthians, inspire a deeper reliance on faith and community support?
4. How has your understanding of God's eternal perspective influenced the way you approach loss and mourning?

CHAPTER 19

Finding Hope in Unexpected Places

"'The Eagles! The Eagles!' he shouted. 'The Eagles are coming!'"[63]
—J. R. R. Tolkien

Sunrise was beginning to peak from behind the morning fog when I first glimpsed their mysterious shadows. Pink and orange beams of light began streaking across the horizon, soothing my icy cheeks as those rusty streaks zoomed past my peripheral vision. I lifted my head towards the frozen canopy of barren trees and observed a

63 Tolkien, J. R. R. *The Hobbit*. HarperCollins, 2012.

medium-sized bird as it landed effortlessly on a dormant moss-covered branch.

As I continued my morning walk with my one-hundred-pound Great Pyrenees, I was suddenly greeted by a sight that filled me with wonder. Dozens of gray-brown, plump, feathered robins with copper bellies were hopping and flying through the sleepy limbs of maple trees lining the street. Bear also noticed their spectral presence and barked as if in welcome.

Robins in January? The early return of these birds was a delightful surprise that filled me with a sense of wonder and hope amidst winter's darkness.

In late December and early January, the Pacific Northwest doesn't see sunrise until around 8 o'clock; consequently, I often start my day in darkness. Not only do I wake up before the sun, but by the winter solstice, sunset comes as early as 4:30 p.m. This means that when I leave work, the sun has already set, and I drive home in the dark as well. With such brief daylight hours, both mornings and evenings feel especially dim. Sometimes, it feels like the day barely gets started before it's already over, and I miss the energy and warmth that sunlight brings to my routine.

With more than sixteen hours of pitch-darkness in a day, it can be easy to lose sight of the light or even forget it existed.

Depression, like a heavy fog, had seeped into my veins unexpectedly after the final explosions of New Year's Eve fireworks disappeared in the night sky, leaving a momentary haze of smoky skeletons levitating in the dark.

The odor of spent pyrotechnics and rotten eggs permeated the landscape, making me think of death again.

I had finally removed the last decorations from the Christmas tree that would be placed on the edge of our street, waiting for the Boy Scouts to pick up its carcass. This year, I decided to put all my son's Christmas ornaments in a separate box from the rest of the Christmas decorations.

It was now the fifth Christmas after Sebastian had died. Twenty-three ornaments, each one representing something that I had deemed significant that had occurred in Sebastian's life the previous year: his first steps, the year he stopped nursing (he was almost three), the year he played the trombone, his driver's license, when he was keeper for his club soccer team, his graduation from high school in 2012, The year he left home to go to college, and the year he spent in rehab.

One of our favorite Christmas traditions included opening the ornament box and remembering the stories attached to each ornament. But for the last few years, I couldn't let myself remember the stories; I didn't want to cry. I hid most of Sebastian's ornaments at the back of the tree to avoid feeling sad, saving thoughts of them until it was time to pack up for next year.

The red plastic ornament box I had purchased from Target was designed to hold up to thirty-five items. As I prepared to put away the Christmas decorations, I found one more ornament of Sebastian's hiding under the tree skirt. I picked it up, fondly remembering why I had chosen this ornament: it was a blond-haired boy catching a soccer ball, and it looked precisely like Sebastian. As I placed it in the box, I once again felt the weight of my grief, the heaviness of each memory, reminding me of the depth of my loss.

There would be no twenty-fourth, twenty-fifth, twenty-sixth, twenty-seventh, or twenty-eighth ornament to put away.

Equally, I found comfort in the memories attached to Sebastian's Christmas ornaments, and our family found solace in our annual marathon watch party of *The Lord of the Rings* movies together every Christmas. The epic journey of Frodo and Sam mirrors our own journey through grief and loss. Every year, we pulled out our special-edition extended versions of the trilogy, which added an extra 2 hours of film footage. Once we found our places on the couch and inserted the first disc into the VCR, we always rooted for Sam and Frodo, hoping they would find their way through the darkness and despair toward the light. Their story became a metaphor for our own, a reminder that even in the darkest of times, there is always the possibility of hope and redemption.

The Great Ring of Sauron had finally been cast into the abyss of the volcano Orodruin, unwittingly by Gollum. The aftermath of its evil poured out of Mount Doom; volcanic ash and lava exploded from its bowels, demolishing the Hobbit's path back home. There would be no happy ending for Frodo and Sam. Frodo told Sam, "We have only a little time to wait now. We are lost in ruin and downfall, and there is no escape."[64] They could go no further. Surrounded by rivers of fire flowing around them and hot cinders falling

---

64 Tolkien, J. R. R. *The Return of the King*. Del Rey, 1986.

from above, they clung to each other on a barren rock, waiting for the darkness to overtake them.

And then, when Frodo and Sam had lost all hope, through the darkness came three colossal eagles to rescue them, taking them back to the light and into a safe place.

Tolkien referred to this part of the story as a *eucatastrophe.* He asserted that all good stories (fairy tales) must have a happy ending.[65] Catastrophe comes from two Greek words, κατα (down or downward) and στρεφπ (I turn). Combined, it originally meant the harrowing end in a Greek tragedy; at first glance, Frodo and Sam's story bears a resemblance to a traditional Greek tragedy.

However, Tolkien does not discount their failures or defeats. As readers, we agonize with Sam and Frodo, wondering how they will escape this mess. We wonder if our heroes will have a happy ending. Will they meet a tragic end in the same manner as their literary Greek heroes did centuries before?

But Tolkien does the unexpected and creates a new word by adding a small Greek word, ευ (good), to the beginning of the catastrophe. The unexpected does happen; a *eucatastrophe* comes in the form of three enormous eagles, Gwaihair, Landroval, and Meneldor the Swift. They came from nowhere, uninvited, and saved Frodo and Sam from darkness and death. The story's direction shifts into something positive, leading the reader to a satisfying and happy ending.

65 Tolkien, J. R. R. *On Fairy-Stories*. HarperCollins, 2014.

The Jewish people had also been waiting for a happy ending in the person of the Messiah. This Messiah was to come and drive out the present Roman authorities when John the Baptist, a cousin of Jesus of Nazareth, was born. John's mother, Elizabeth, had been unable to get pregnant. An infertile woman during this time was considered an outcast; it was an indication of some divine disfavor and brought dishonor to the family. We don't know why Elizabeth was unable to have children. She may have been in menopause or had some other medical condition that caused her infertility. Nevertheless, we know the Bible declared she was "righteous in the sight of God, observing all the Lord's commands and decrees blamelessly" (Luke 1:6).

Then, a *eucatastrophe* happened while John's father was working in the Temple of Herod. An angel of the Lord appeared and told him that Elizabeth was to have a baby, even in her old age. His name was to be John, and he would be filled with the Holy Spirit, helping to bring people back to God (Luke 1:5–17).

It seemed that after 400 years of silence, God's people would hear his voice again.

The Bible says that after John reached adulthood, he emerged from the wilderness, bursting through the silence and bringing not a sword but words of repentance; the world was ready for a change. He came to prepare people and gave them a glimpse of spring. John came to bring hope to a darkened world. Like a robin in January, John was not the light (or the spring), but he came as a witness to the coming light (John 1:8).

The prophet Zechariah stated that John would play an essential role in the future, comparing his significance to that of a robin in January, which signals changes ahead even if they are not immediately apparent.

> And you, my child, will be called a prophet of the Most High;
> for you will go before the Lord to prepare the way for him,
> to give his people the knowledge of salvation
> through the forgiveness of their sins,
> because of the tender mercy of our God,
> by which the rising sun will come to us from heaven
> to shine on those living in darkness
> and in the shadow of death,
> to guide our feet into the path of peace (Luke 1:76–79).

The birth of Jesus was the ultimate *eucatastrophic* event.

In his incarnation, Jesus voluntarily became like us, born to an unwed teenager, to live among us, who experienced all the joys, hurts, and pains of a human being. Jesus got tired, thirsty, and hungry, and wept for his dead friend. Because Jesus was tempted and suffered, Jesus knows our pain. At the same time, Jesus is God; he was at the beginning when God created the world. Jesus cares about his creation, and though he had no sin, he took our sin upon Himself and died on the cross. “But God demonstrates his own love for us in this: While we were still sinners, Christ died for us” (Romans 5:8).

After Jesus' death, his disciples went into hiding, scared that the ones who killed their friend would also try to kill them since they were his followers. They had lost sight of the light. Jesus had died, and now they were lost in their grief. They had not yet realized that the ultimate *eucatastrophe* had already occurred.

They needed to see Jesus and have their happy ending.

Jesus' death on the cross was intended to be another disaster story for humankind. Satan used evil men to kill Jesus. Tolkien called this a *dyscatastrophe,* δυσ (bad, ill, hard, difficult);[66] instead, Satan defeated himself when Jesus defeated death by rising from the dead. The *eucatastrophe* of the resurrection offers the most incredible happy ending possible, demonstrating that evil and death cannot prevail.

Bear barked, and the robins squawked and flew through the mist. Sunbeams sparkled like emeralds on their wings, and their upbeat songs reverberated down the street. I smiled. Robins are a type of *eucatastrophe;* they give glimmers of hope. It means that spring is around the corner, even though it's still winter. Before the crocuses and daffodils begin to peek through the still-frozen soil, when depression overwhelms me, the loss of my son envelopes my mind once again, and the robin's unexpected arrival gives me a glimmer of what is yet to come. Robins let us know the light is coming. Every day, there will be more and more light with each passing twenty-four hours until there is more light in the day than darkness. Then we know spring has arrived.

66 Tolkien, J. R. R. *On Fairy-Stories*. HarperCollins, 2014.

Jesus is my ultimate hope in the darkest part of winter. He reminds me, in Him, that my spring is always coming, and death is not the end.

One day, when it is my turn to die and leave this earth, I, by faith, will finally see Jesus face to face, standing with outstretched arms, welcoming me home. There will be many others who have gone before me, including Sebastian, waiting to see my homecoming, but then it will no longer matter.

There will be no more tears, no more mourning, only Jesus.

Jesus always gives me hope.

THOUGHTS TO CONSIDER

1. How does the concept of a "*eucatastrophe*," as described in this chapter, resonate with your own experiences of finding hope during difficult times?
2. In Tolkien's narrative, the arrival of the eagles symbolizes unexpected salvation. Can you recall a time in your life when help or hope came from an unexpected source?
3. What parallels can be drawn between the biblical accounts of John the Baptist and Jesus' resurrection and the idea of finding light in the darkness presented in this chapter?
4. The chapter discusses robins as a metaphor for hope during winter. In your own life, what symbols or signs have served as reminders of hope after the loss of a child?
5. How does reflecting on the ultimate hope offered by God, as illustrated in the resurrection of Jesus, influence the way you approach grief and loss?

CHAPTER 20

Peace and Contentment in Our Messy Mourning

"The Lord said to Moses on Mount Sinai, "Speak to the Israelites and say to them: 'When you enter the land I am going to give, the land itself must observe a sabbath to the Lord. For six years sow your fields, and for six years prune your vineyards and gather their crops. But in the seventh year the land is to have a sabbath of rest, a sabbath to the Lord..."

—Leviticus 25:1–4

2024 marked the seventh anniversary of Sebastian's death.

Therefore, on his death anniversary in September, we, as a family, traveled to Tucson, Arizona, and as a result, we were able to eat at Sweet Tomatoes. This all-you-can-eat salad buffet restaurant chain recently reopened after the COVID-19 pandemic forced the bankruptcy and closure of all ninety-seven of its locations, including the one in Vancouver, where we lived. It was our favorite restaurant when my children were growing up.

It made sense to go to Sweet Tomatoes for numerous reasons.

For many years, Steve and I had our regular Friday date nights at this restaurant. We'd fill up on the all-you-can-eat salad and discuss how our week was going.

Isabel's first job, when she was eighteen, was at Sweet Tomatoes. She learned to make salads and would continually fill up all the containers with freshly cut fruits and salad toppings. Steve and I loved to go in and watch her work. She, on the other hand, did not appreciate our presence.

When Sebastian and Isabel were toddlers, Sweet Tomatoes offered "Kids Under Two Eat Free" menus. It was a fantastic place to get a variety of healthy vegetables and fruits, plus their favorite mac and cheese and self-serve ice cream. They loved going to Sweet Tomatoes.

I also had my share of "bad mom" moments at Sweet Tomatoes. Once Sebastian complained that he couldn't eat his broccoli.

"Momma, I can't eat it. My tummy hurts." Sebastian's tummy was always hurting, especially when he didn't want to eat certain foods.

Using my firm mom voice, I said, "You will eat your broccoli, or you won't get any ice cream." I pointed to the broccoli in question on his plate and said sternly, "Eat it."

But I can't, Momma," He whined, "I don't feel good."

You were fine three minutes ago. Eat your broccoli."

"OK," he said, begrudgingly. As he slowly picked up the broccoli and put it in his mouth, he began to gag dramatically. Then he proceeded to vomit the broccoli and what seemed to be the entire contents of his stomach onto his plate and across the table.

There was something significant about what was happening in year seven; a shift in my grief had started to take place. Seven years is often seen as a milestone in many cultures. For me, it marked a turning point where my grief began to transform into acceptance. I've noticed over the past seven years that my grief has evolved and changed; my emotions are not all over the place, and I'm not crying like I used to. It's not that I'm 'over' the loss of Sebastian, but I'm learning to live with it differently. I'm unexpectedly at peace and grateful for where I am now. This transformation may offer a beacon of hope for anyone experiencing similar pain.

In the second chapter of Genesis, after spending six days creating the earth, the stars, the sun, plants, the animals, and humans, God "rested from all his work" on the seventh day (Genesis 2:2). In the same way, as rest was essential after creation, allowing time for rest is vital for those grieving, as it provides space for emotional and physical healing. Rest is not only a fundamental component that enables the body to heal, especially after the trauma of losing a child by suicide, but it is also essential to heal and repair our broken hearts. It is necessary to give ourselves permission to rest and recover during such a challenging time, recognizing that taking this time is not only necessary but also life-changing, as we begin to see God's goodness and beauty in our lives once again.

This concept of the seventh day as a time of rest is deeply woven into the fabric of biblical teaching. Throughout the scriptures, God commanded his followers to rest from their work on the seventh day. When they entered the land that God had promised his people, God commanded them to work for six days and then rest on the seventh day.

The Sabbath, observed every seventh day (typically Sunday in the United States), is not only a command to cease from work but also a way to see God's provisions for us, to pause and allow for spiritual, emotional, and physical renewal. Resting can revive our souls and heal our emotional wounds. By allowing ourselves to rest, we can acknowledge our limitations, which in turn allows for more space for grieving, reflection, and connection with God.

Beyond the weekly Sabbath, the Hebrew Scriptures also describe a deeper rhythm of rest and renewal in the seventh year, known as the Sabbatical Year or the Year of Jubilee (Leviticus 25:8, 10–17). These seven-year cycles (every fifty years) allowed the Israelites a time of liberation, restoration, and celebration. God's people were commanded to let the land rest, to refrain from sowing or harvesting, and to trust him to provide for their needs. People's debts were forgiven, enslaved people were freed, and land that had been sold was returned to its original owners. The Year of Jubilee was a powerful symbol of ultimate healing, redemption, and the restoration of broken relationships and communities. This act of faith was a tangible expression of dependence on God and a reminder that true healing and provision come from Him.

In the context of grief, reaching the seventh year can represent a significant milestone, a period when the heart and soul may begin to experience a new kind of rest, a shift from acute pain to a gentler, more sustainable way of living with loss.

For those who are grieving the loss of a child by suicide, the seventh year can feel like a mini-Jubilee, a time when the intense sorrow and turmoil of earlier years begin to give way to peace, release, and even a sense of renewal. It is as if the soul, after years of laboring under this weight of intense loss, is finally able to rest. Finally, the promise of Jubilee reminds us that restoration is possible, that God's love can transform even the deepest wounds into sources of peace and hope.

Therefore, comparable to the year of Jubilee, which marked a time of restoration and renewed hope, I found reminders of this restoration during our visit to the newly opened Sweet Tomatoes restaurant. As we entered the newly opened restaurant, we were overwhelmed by a multitude of memories, both good and bad. Yet, our shared laughter, the comfort of familiar foods, and the joy of being together as a family allowed those feelings of sorrow to give way to a new sense of belonging.

We grabbed our trays and began placing all the delicious veggies and salad fixings on our plates. It was strange being here without Sebastian, but after we sat down and started eating, the stories of our life with Sebastian flowed easily from our lips.

"Sebastian would have loved coming here." Isabel blurted out, "Even if the bacon bits are fake (when she had worked there, they were real!)." There were tears in her eyes, as there were tears in Steve's eyes. The anecdotes continued; every time we got the focaccia bread, the soft-serve ice cream, a drink, or the red Jell-O, a story would emerge. We laughed, then Steve or Isabel would share another story.

And I felt an unexpected peace, a rest, that I hadn't felt for a long time; a peace I never thought I'd feel again. A peace that seemed to surpass all understanding. Jesus promised us this peace. "Peace I leave with you; my peace I give you. I do not give to you as the world gives. Do not let your hearts be troubled and do not be afraid" (John 14:27).

Who knew that in a restaurant with a red tomato carpet, I would sense a calmness and contentment with my life? In a horrible moment seven years earlier, my life had changed. I thought I'd never be the same, and I'm not.

But I am changed, and who knew, in some ways, for the better?

Tim Keller wrote:

> Suffering puts its fingers on good things that have become too important to us. We must respond to suffering not ordinarily by jettisoning those loved things but by turning to God and loving him more and

> putting our roots down deeper into him. You will never really understand your heart when things are going well. It is only when things go badly that you can truly see them. And that's because it is only when suffering comes that you realize who is the true God and what are the false gods of our lives. Only the true God can go with you through the furnace and out to the other side.[67]

When I heard God's voice on that Oregon beach many years ago, I had to trust Him no matter what, and that I had to lay Sebastian on God's altar. Abraham, in the same way, had to trust God and lay his son Isaac on an altar. Little did I know that I would soon embark on this journey. I certainly wouldn't have chosen this path for anyone. I never want another child to die by suicide, or cancer, or through an accident. But I do know that with everything I have faced and will face in the future, God holds me in the palm of His hand, and He will continue to care for me in my darkest places. He has given me peace that surpasses all understanding. "Cast your cares on the Lord and he will sustain you; he will never let the righteous be shaken" (Psalm 55:22).

God will never let us go. We don't need to be afraid to cling to Him in our pain, suffering, and messy mourning. Throughout our suffering, we are being refined and being made more perfect until we finally meet Jesus face to face. After the unimaginable loss of losing a child, the journey of grief can be both deeply traumatic and, at the same time,

---

67 Keller, Timothy. *Walking with God through Pain and Suffering*. Penguin Books, 2015.

transformative. At first, the pain seems insurmountable; each day is a challenge to get out of bed. Yet, over time, the grief process can slowly mold us in ways we never imagined. Who knew that in some ways grief could be good? As we move forward in our grief, we may begin to discover new qualities of strength and resilience within ourselves. Our perspectives will begin to shift; we now learn to appreciate small, seemingly insignificant matters such as stars in the winter evening sky, laughter shared over a meal, or fond memories recalled with loved ones. The things I used to worry about are no longer a concern. Grief forces us to reevaluate what is important and teaches us to root ourselves more deeply in God's love.

In time, the brokenness of grief can become a source of unexpected beauty. This transformation will be subtle, yet it is ongoing. With each step, God holds us close, guiding us toward greater wholeness until, one day, we are reunited with our loved ones in His presence.

THOUGHTS TO CONSIDER

1. What role do shared family anecdotes and memories play in the healing process?
2. The author quotes John 14:27 and Psalm 55:22. How do these biblical passages deepen your understanding of your spiritual journey? What do they reveal about the relationship between faith and emotional healing?
3. Tim Keller is quoted as saying, "Suffering puts its fingers on good things that have become too important to us." How does this perspective resonate with or challenge your own understanding of the purpose of suffering?
4. How does the concept of "beauty in brokenness" apply to the author's journey? Can you identify moments where this theme is evident in your own challenges?
5. The author mentions that through suffering, we are being refined. In what ways can challenges in life create opportunities for personal or spiritual growth?

CHAPTER 21

How to Help (and Not to Help) Someone Grieving the Loss of a Child by Suicide

"Aren't all these notes the senseless writings of a man who won't accept the fact that there is nothing we can do with suffering except to suffer it?"[68]

—C. S. Lewis

[68] Lewis, C.S. *A Grief Observed.* HarperOne, 2015.

Journal entry—A letter unsent:

January 2018

Dear (blank),

I read your Facebook post today. You were sharing your joy because a year ago, your son had tried to kill himself. He eventually recovered, got better, and is now married. You ended your post with "I have a smile on my face because my son lives."

And yet, my son is still dead.

I also remember that day a year ago. You had frantically texted me while I was working, wanting to talk. Our boys had been childhood friends. You told me your son had attempted suicide and desperately needed help. I remember reeling back in a panic, my heart started racing, and my hands were sweaty while reading your text, because it had only been thirty-three days since my son Sebastian had died by suicide, and yet, you wanted me to help you? I couldn't help myself. How could I help you? I had paced all around the parking lot during lunch that day, trying to figure out what to say. I called Steve and asked him what I should say. I didn't know what to say. I was still too raw and barely functioning. I prayed to God every day that I wouldn't kill someone in my practice as I cared for them. I was a mess.

When you finally called me, you were in a panic. Your son was still in the hospital. You wanted me to fly out and talk to your son. You told me he wouldn't speak to you. You thought I could talk to him. He might have listened to me because of what had happened to my son.

What was I going to say to her son? "Don't kill yourself, look at what Sebastian did?" "You have so much to live for?" My heart ached for your mother's heart and for myself. I understood too deeply how you felt; I had walked in your shoes only a month earlier.

I remember telling you the one thing I had learned thus far through Sebastian's death was that I had to hold on to my children loosely and hold onto God tightly.

I didn't see your son. I couldn't see him. I heard he eventually did get better, and now everything is well for you. I am happy for you, but I am angry with you, my friend. In your happiness, you forgot me, you forgot my loss, you forgot my boy, my boy who is not alive, and you forgot my heart is still broken. My body is slowly healing as well, and I'm learning to move forward one small step at a time, but I am not well yet. I am still clinging to God tightly, not because my son lives but because God's son died for me.

In your happiness, don't forget I was there for you, and my son is still dead.

Jackie

Right after Sebastian's death, well-intentioned friends and family members began to contact me asking for help with their children who were struggling with suicidal thoughts or other mental health issues. At the same time, other well-intentioned acquaintances were offering words of advice or encouragement that sometimes proved unhelpful. Many of these truisms have been discussed in previous chapters. Over the years, after conversing with other mothers who have faced similar losses, it became evident that many of these grieving mothers received presumably well-meaning advice, articles, and books that inadvertently induced further pain.

Looking back on these personal experiences, I began to see how grief is not only painful on its own but can also be made more complicated by the words and actions of others. The above journal entry shows that, even when friends mean well or are themselves hurting, what they say or do can sometimes unknowingly deepen the heartache of losing a child to suicide. In sharing these moments, I hope to highlight the complex emotions that accompany mourning and, at the same time, to remind us of the importance of approaching others' pain with genuine empathy and sensitivity.

It is important to note that most people do not intentionally seek to offend those who are in mourning. Often, awkward statements arise from a person's unsureness about what to say, combined with an innate need to express something to demonstrate sympathy. While the original objective is to offer comfort and support, such interactions can sometimes unintentionally exacerbate the messy mourning process for those who are grieving.

Similarly, it is crucial for those of us who are grieving to extend compassion towards individuals attempting to support us. It is natural to feel irritation and distress from these "well-meaning" statements during the early stages of our grief. However, it is essential to remember that our friends and family members are doing their best and may not fully understand our current state of mourning. In my personal experience, it is particularly relevant in cases involving loss due to suicide. C. S. Lewis, reflecting on the loss of his wife Joy, once wrote, "I see people, as they approach me, trying to make up their minds whether they'll 'say something about it' or not. I hate if they do and if they don't."[69]

With this in mind, I have listed twelve ways friends, family, and acquaintances can help those who are grieving. This list is not exhaustive, but it may be a helpful tool when encouraging and serving those affected by the loss of a child.

1. Pray without ceasing. Nothing else is more important than praying for those who are hurting. Plan on praying for these hurting people for years to come. As I have mentioned, grief can last for a long time; everyone needs prayer. Your consistent prayers can be a source of comfort and strength. "...The prayer of a righteous person is powerful and effective" (James 5:16).
2. Try to listen without offering commentary on your own life or the lives of others. Try not to make comparisons unless you have lost a child to suicide as well. (I once had a friend who told me they understood my sorrow because they had lost their dog.) "My dear brothers and sisters, take note of this: Everyone should be quick to listen, slow to speak, and slow to become angry" (James 1:19).
3. If you can, send cards, emails, texts, and messages. Even though we might not respond to them, they do

[69] Lewis, C. S. *A Grief Observed.* HarperOne, 2015.

mean a lot. My friend Lisa sent me cards a few times a month for over a year. I still have them.

4. Help with practical chores. Be specific. "Let me do this for you." "I want to mow your grass. How about tomorrow? Avoid asking, "Is there anything I can do?" People in early grief often struggle to articulate their needs and may claim they are fine when, in reality, they are not.
5. Make phone calls for those who are grieving. Be available to make appointments, pick up people, and run errands. I accompanied my friend to her lawyer to offer support as she was trying to settle her estate. Simply being available and being supportive means a lot.
6. Admit that you don't know what someone is going through (unless you have experienced it yourself), but you still want to help.
7. Offer support throughout the grieving process, rather than offering quick solutions. There are no quick solutions. Grief takes time, longer than most people realize or acknowledge.
8. Avoid obvious cliches; avoid statements like, "It was their time to go," "Everything happens for a reason," or "God doesn't give anything we can't handle." We can't handle this; that is why we need God. It is better to say nothing and look at numbers 1 and 2 again.
9. Go out for coffee or take a walk. Offer to walk a grieving person's dog, change litter boxes, or take

animals to their vet appointments. Sometimes, it might be better to say, "How about Wednesday at 10:00?" Having too many options can lead to even more confusion. Keep choices simple for a time.

10. Avoid asking someone who is grieving, "How are you doing?" The reality is that most grieving people are not doing well, and this question can be difficult for them to answer honestly. Many individuals in grief hesitate to share their true feelings, fearing they may be a burden or worried about being pitied and misunderstood. For those wanting to support someone who is grieving, it's important to acknowledge that the struggle may last much longer than expected. Offering ongoing support and reassurance can be especially meaningful during this time.

    Let those who are grieving know you are thinking of them or keeping them in your thoughts and prayers, depending on what feels appropriate for their beliefs. When I do pray for people, I usually let them know, often with a text. I have never had anyone tell me I didn't need to pray for them. We all need prayer.

11. Be patient. Grief is not easy, and no two people grieve in the same way. It may take a while before a person is ready to "face the world" once again. Again, #1 is helpful in this regard.

12. Try not to ask, "How did it happen? or "How did they do it?" or "Why would they do such a thing to you?" Our Western culture, for some reason, wants to know "all the details." We are curious, but

it's not appropriate to ask such questions unless the grieving person initiates the conversation by sharing their thoughts first. It can be insensitive, and it will always be hard to discuss (I still struggle to talk about the actual details). In the end, it doesn't matter or bring one's child back.

By practicing these twelve supportive actions, we can make a meaningful difference in the life of someone who is grieving the loss of a child by suicide or other traumatic death. Simple gestures, such as sending messages, helping with chores, walking a dog, and offering quiet companionship, can show that we care and provide comfort during this difficult time. Avoiding clichés and being patient helps create a safe space for mourning. Taking the initiative to support, listening without judgment, and consistently offering practical assistance can ease the burden of grief and help foster healing, reminding those who are grieving that they are valued and supported for as long as they need. Most importantly, praying for them every day and letting them know, either by text, letter, phone call, or in person, this spiritual support allows those who are grieving to know they are not alone.

THOUGHTS TO CONSIDER

1. How can offering prayer and spiritual support be beneficial for individuals in the early stages of grief?
2. What are some practical ways to listen and provide comfort to someone who is grieving?
3. Why might common phrases like "It was their time to go" or "Everything happens for a reason" be harmful to someone experiencing loss?
4. How can practical acts of service, such as running errands or helping with chores, impact the grieving process
5. What are some long-term approaches to supporting a grieving friend or family member beyond the immediate aftermath of loss?

Epilogue

Beauty in My Brokenness

"'I wish it need not have happened in my time,' said Frodo. 'So do I,' said Gandalf, 'and so do all who live to see such times. But that is not for them to decide. All we have to decide is what to do with the time that is given us.'"[70]

—J. R .R. Tolkien

"Mom. Could you get me a pair of Ray-Bans for Christmas?"

Sebastian sounded happier on the phone, more like his usual self. For the last seven weeks, he had been in Phoenix, Arizona, confined to an inpatient rehab center for addiction. Rehab was not the place I had expected Sebastian

70 Tolkien, J. R. R. *The Fellowship of the Ring*. HarperCollins, 1991.

to end up. I had hopes and dreams for him; I had his future all planned out. He was intelligent and curious, but after quitting his college soccer team and dropping out of school, I watched him spiral out of control as he self-medicated with marijuana and other drugs that helped enhance his destructive habits. Somehow, Sebastian had lost sight of the ambitions he once had. His poor choices, along with ignoring the warnings of those who cared for him, led him down a path he could never have imagined for himself. Now Sebastian's days were spent learning how not to be an addict with a bunch of other men in similar circumstances.

"Not the aviator kind. I want the black Wayfarers. All the guys here have them."

"I could do that," I told him during our weekly hour-long phone visit.

Therefore, I bought Sebastian those exact sunglasses and gave them to him for Christmas, hoping they could help him heal in some way and continue to keep him safe. My thoughts at this time were that if I gave him gifts and presents that kept his spirits up, he wouldn't be too depressed in this facility. I had hoped he'd finish this program and then we'd get him back on a track with his life once again.

I thought he would be safe in rehab. If I didn't know where he was, I'd worry he might be dead. Sleeping was brutal on the nights I didn't know where he was. I spent many long hours praying to God in the dark. I couldn't do anything else.

Ray-Ban Wayfarers have been the epitome of cool for generations. Sebastian always wanted to be seen as cool, even in rehab. Bausch and Lomb initially designed these black trapezoidal plastic frames in the 1950s. In the 60s, they graced the faces of celebrities such as Bob Dylan, John F. Kennedy, and Andy Warhol. In the 1980s, they were featured in over sixty movies, including Tom Cruise's *Risky Business*, John Belushi's *The Blues Brothers,* and John Hughes' film *The Breakfast Club.* Most recently, Daniel Craig wore them during his reign as James Bond.

It has been said that the eyes are the window to the soul. In that case, Wayfarer's opaque lenses are perfect at concealing what is going on in the mind of the individual who wears them. It's as if they are a piece of armor protecting a warrior from harm. Removing them makes one vulnerable to attack or pity.

In the same way as a knight dons his armor before heading into battle, shielding his body from the arrows and blows of an unpredictable world, the dark, stylish frames of Wayfarer sunglasses become a modern suit of protection. Behind their glossy surface, a person can hide fear, pain, or uncertainty, presenting instead a façade of confidence and coolness. The sunglasses allow the wearer to control what is revealed and what remains hidden, almost like a protective shell that separates the fragile self from the judgment and scrutiny of others.

I never saw Sebastian wearing his Wayfarers. Still, I suspected he put them on in front of a mirror and practiced wearing them before going out in public. He did something like this during his teenage years after watching the movie *Zoolander.* He spent hours perfecting his "blue steel" pose made famous by Ben Stiller. I have hundreds of self-portraits Sebastian took, saved on my desktop computer, of him sucking in his cheekbones and pursing his lips in pursuit of that iconic look.

Sebastian had been in Phoenix for five months the first time he attempted to kill himself. One morning after eating breakfast, he walked away into the hot Arizona sun from a rehabilitation program for teens and adults struggling with addictions and disappeared for twenty-four hours. He tried to hang himself with a rope he had kept hidden away. Fortunately for me, the rope broke. He spent three weeks in a psychiatric hospital and started taking antipsychotic medications. After that, we moved Sebastian to Bend, Oregon. This treatment program was closer to home, and they could help him with his medications. He found a therapist, and I visited him every couple of weeks.

"I'm bored, Mom. I can't do this any longer." Sebastian had whined to me during one of our last phone calls.

"It's only for three more months," I told him. "You can do this. I know you can. Then you can come home."

"I'm tired of working in the thrift store all day."

"Not every job is exciting. Why don't you organize the books? It will keep your brain busy until I can come visit again."

A week after Sebastian died, I found his sunglasses hidden amongst his personal belongings at the bottom of a broken packing box. The homeless shelter where he stayed for only one night sent it to me. One container held everything he owned. He had been kicked out of his rehabilitation program the day before. Sebastian had completed nine months, but the director said he wouldn't follow the rules anymore.

Staying at the shelter was supposed to be temporary, thirty days, according to what the director told us. After that, he thought Sebastian would appreciate how effective the rehabilitation program had been for him.

The night Sebastian died, he asked, "I can't come home, can I, Mom?"

"I wish you could," I replied. But I knew I still couldn't trust Sebastian. I wanted to, but I couldn't yet.

"It's OK. Mom. I understand." He said quietly. "I love you."

"I love you too," I whispered back. "I'll see you next week."

But there was no next week.

When Sebastian was fourteen, I heard God say, "Jackie, are you willing to lay Sebastian on my altar?" I twirled around to make sure there was no one around me speaking. I had been walking by myself one early morning on a deserted Oregon beach while squawking seagulls flew over my head. What did that even mean, "lay Sebastian on the altar?" I remembered that God spoke to Abraham in this way. God had tested Abraham and told him to take his only son, Isaac, and sacrifice him on Mt. Moriah. Abraham obeyed God even though it meant his son might die. As he raised his knife to slay his son, an angel of God stopped him and said, "...Now I know that you fear God because you have not withheld from me your son, your only son" Genesis 22:12).

Was God testing me like He tested Abraham? Hadn't I already been through enough pain in my life? Now God wanted me to "give away" my only son. Then I remembered that God had given up his only son. Could I do this? I only had Sebastian for fourteen years. I had plans for him. I wasn't ready yet. As the wind whipped my hair across my face, I stopped walking and stood still on the beach. I stared into the sun overhead, my eyes swelling with tears, and then I asked, "What if you don't give Sebastian back?"

The waves crashed against my bare feet, and the seagulls continued to scream around my head. Then, similarly, as God spoke to Moses through a burning bush, I heard God roar through the ocean wind and say, "You have to trust me."

For nine years, I pondered the meaning of those words. Each time I faced uncertainty about Sebastian's future, this memory returned, sometimes quietly, other times with the force of that original ocean gust. I realized it wasn't about giving Sebastian away in a physical sense; God wasn't asking me to abandon my son or relinquish my love for him. Instead, I began to understand that the true sacrifice was letting go of the dreams and expectations I had built around Sebastian; my hopes for his future, my plans for his happiness, all the wishes that belonged to me rather than to him. I struggled with the idea that my own desires might cloud what was truly best for Sebastian, and that trust meant releasing my grip on those dreams and allowing God's purposes to unfold, whatever they might be. This lesson grew gradually within me, becoming clearer with each passing year and every trial, no matter how difficult they were, they taught me that genuine faith is found not in clinging, but in letting go, even when the outcome was painfully uncertain.

A week after Sebastian died, I once again remembered this conversation with God, and I finally understood what God had been trying to say. It wasn't about Sebastian after all. It was about me trusting God, no matter what happened. In that moment of grief, I felt God's presence wash over me and fill my heart, and I clung to Him, cried to Him, prayed to Him, and trusted Him to get me through this horrible pain that overwhelmed me.

I had no choice. I had nowhere else to go but to Him.

Two years after Sebastian passed away, I looked out the kitchen window of my rental apartment on the south end of Lake Wakatipu. I witnessed the first glimpses of dawn peeking from behind the mountains. The Remarkables, a majestic and ruggedly resplendent mountain range, appeared to wrap its ancient rocklike arms around the nearby towns of Frankton and Queenstown. The indigenous Māori people, who first inhabited Aotearoa (present-day New Zealand) in the 13th century, called the Remarkables *Kawarau,* named after an ancient, esteemed Māori chief. *Kawa* means bitter or pointed, and *rau* means many or more than 100.[71] The Maori name aptly described the numerous jagged razor-sharp peaks I observed over the past week; these pointed pinnacles appeared to pierce the pervading blue skies across the New Zealand landscape.

71 "More Than a Name: The Stories Behind Your Favorite Mountain Peaks." *Red Bull*, Red Bull Media House, https://www.redbull.com/nz-en/summit-challenge-lake-wakatipu

The Remarkables, running north to south along the South Island, seem as if it were a sleeping giant's backbone. It contains some of the world's most photogenic alpine scenery, mingled with snowcapped fjords, flower-filled pine forests and meadows, drinkable freshwater rivers and lakes, numerous waterfalls, and beautiful, quaint towns enveloped within its vast wilderness.

God knew I needed beauty today.

It was during one of our LOTR marathons that we began to fall in love with the landscape of New Zealand. Peter Jackson filmed many scenes in and around The Remarkables, a rugged mountainous area near Queenstown on the South Island. Since our family loved all things J.R.R. Tolkien, it didn't surprise us when Isabel announced during a family trip to New Mexico that she thought God wanted her to go to New Zealand. At the age of twenty, Isabel was in a dark place, trying to figure out who she was. She had dropped out of art school the year before and struggled with severe anxiety. She left the United States to search for her own "Middle-earth." I thought she'd call me in a week to fly to New Zealand and take her back home.

Instead, Isabel spent three and a half years in New Zealand. Not only did she find her "Middle-earth," but more importantly, she found herself. My daughter blossomed and matured as she immersed herself on the shores of Lake Wakatipu. In this place, she experienced the love of Jesus in a new and personal way, apart from her parents' views of Christianity. Isabel made her profession of faith public at her baptism in those cold waters, along with her future husband, Brennan, an exceptional young man from Canada who shared her love for Jesus.

Isabel felt compelled to come home from New Zealand after Sebastian's first suicide attempt. She hadn't seen her brother in almost a year, and she felt enormously far away while he was struggling, which weighed heavily on her heart. The pain of knowing Sebastian was facing such difficult times created a sense of urgency and helplessness that she couldn't ignore.

After Sebastian's death, the grief became almost unbearable for Isabel. The loss shaped her decision to marry Brennan, who became a source of comfort and stability during her darkest days. Their marriage allowed Isabel to navigate the deep sorrow and confusion that followed her brother's death.

Isabel and Brennan returned to New Zealand immediately after the first anniversary of Sebastian's passing. The move felt bittersweet for all of us. I didn't want her to be that far away, and yet I somehow knew she longed for the familiar landscapes that had once brought her peace.

For this reason, while Isabel and Brennan were living in Queenstown, it only made sense then that we would end up in New Zealand on Sebastian's second anniversary.

Mourning is messy.

After finding Sebastian's sunglasses, I began wearing them every day. I wore them on sunny days, cloudy days, and rainy days. They hid my swollen eyes from lack of sleep, from the recurring nightmares I had of Sebastian falling off that cliff.

He died alone without me by his side.

I wore his glasses in every Facebook and Instagram photo I shared. Sebastian's glasses developed special powers and seemed to protect me and keep me safe. They provided the façade of seemingly everyday life, a life that appeared to be moving forward. Yet, no one looking at those photos knew the sunglasses belonged to him.

Every day, I'd check for them before I left the house. I knew them by feeling as I dug into the dark cavern of my purse. Panic would well up in the mornings if I couldn't find them. But as soon as I touched them, my brain would calm down, and I could go on with my day. It was as if, in those sunglasses, I had a part of Sebastian with me all the time. They provided comfort and a sense of stability.

Sebastian's sunglasses have traveled with me around the world. They've seen the WWI trenches in France, walked the streets of London, and visited the places where J.R.R. Tolkien and C.S. Lewis met to discuss the books they were writing. They've traversed the Swiss Alps by train, listening to the cowbells in the mountains' grassy fields. They've navigated the streets of Jerusalem, listening to the Muslim call to worship. They've seen the cities where Jesus performed most of his miracles. At every location, I'd say, "Sebastian would have loved this place."

Finally, in New Zealand, they visited Sebastian's sister, and we searched for Middle-earth.

It was Isabel's idea. "Let's take Sebastian's ashes up into the Remarkables," she mentioned on Facebook Messenger a few months before we came to visit.

Sebastian's ashes sat on a bookshelf in his former bedroom, next to the makeshift memorial of mementos I had gathered over the past twenty months. I'd find something of his randomly around the house, a sock, a picture, his wallet, and my heart would start to race again; the tears would well up, and I'd quickly take that newfound keepsake and place it next to his white plastic urn, then close the door, leaving it for another day.

"He never got to come to New Zealand." She added. "I think he would have loved it here."

"I think you are right," I replied.

Sebastian's birth was supposed to be the *pièce de resistance* of my "and they lived happily ever after" story.

I've since learned there is no really happily ever after on this side of heaven.

The Apostle John wrote, "A woman giving birth to a child has pain because her time has come; but when her baby is born, she forgets the anguish because of her joy that a child is born into the world" (John 16:21). Birth pains are the promise of what is yet to come. They announce the end is near. Once we hold our newborn baby, the pain becomes a memory, replaced by joy, happiness, and a profound love we didn't know we'd have for another human being.

But in Genesis, God told Eve, after she had disobeyed Him by eating forbidden fruit, "I will make your pains in childbearing severe; with painful labor you give birth to children..." (Genesis 3:16). Our pastor once explained that a mother continues to have "pain" after childbirth as she raises her children. Mothers worry about their children: worry if they are safe, worry that they eat enough, worry that they don't eat enough, worry that their child might make the slightest cough in the middle of the night. Worry they might die. The pain of mothering never stops, even as our children reach adulthood. It is always painful. It continues to hurt.

We drove high up into the Remarkables and found a spot off the road to park. There was no one else nearby. Here we climbed a well-trodden path that led to a rocky ridge. We reached the edge of the precipice as the sun began to set over Lake Wakatipu; its red, yellow, and orange hues slowly brightened the dark rocks surrounding us, warming us as if it knew why we were there. Steve uncorked the wine he had brought and poured a glass for Isabel and Brennan. I drank my usual iced tea. Brennan unpackaged the cheese and crackers, and we sat next to each other on a blanket, munching and drinking, watching the sun descend behind the Remarkables as if we had no care in the world. Isabel set down her glass on the blanket, pulled out her phone, scrolled through her playlist, and found the melodious violin strings of Howard Shore's musical score from *The Lord of the Rings* and played "Concerning Hobbits." I was momentarily blinded when my eyes began to fill with tears. I blinked, and as my vision cleared, I drank in the beauty of the Remarkables at sunset. This is why we had come.

"I want to read something from the Bible," Isabel announced. She jumped up from the blanket and scrolled through her phone again. "This Psalm always reminds me of Sebastian." She began to read Psalm 139:

> You have searched me, Lord,
> and you know me.
> You know when I sit and when I rise;
> you perceive my thoughts from afar.
> You discern my going out and my lying down;
> you are familiar with all my ways.
> Before a word is on my tongue
> you, Lord, know it completely (Psalm 139:1–4).

Steve grabbed my hand and squeezed it until it hurt. I could see the tears falling down his face from behind his sunglasses. My tears streamed down my cheeks behind the sunglasses that once belonged to Sebastian. Isabel continued,

> Where can I go from your Spirit?
> Where can I flee from your presence?
> If I go up to the heavens, you are there;
> if I make my bed in the depths, you are there.
> If I say, "Surely the darkness will hide me
> and the light become night around me,"
> even the darkness will not be dark to you;
> the night will shine like the day,
> for darkness is as light to you.
> For you created my inmost being.
> you knit me together in my mother's womb (Psalm 139:7—-13).

Brennan's eyes focused on a blade of grass he was twirling with his fingers. He had never met Sebastian. Sebastian had fallen, slipped off another mountain, and died the day before Brennan was to meet him. Isabel had been thoroughly excited about Brennan meeting her brother. It was all planned, but Sebastian had made other plans.

> I praise you because I am fearfully and wonderfully made;
> your works are wonderful,
> I know that full well.
> My frame was not hidden from you
> when I was made in the secret place,
> when I was woven together in the depths of the earth.
> Your eyes saw my unformed body;
> all the days ordained for me were written in your book
> before one of them came to be (Psalm 139:14–16).

My brain wandered back to two years earlier; Steve, Isabel, and I had agonized about what to put on Sebastian's headstone, something we never thought we'd be doing. We selected a spot underneath a tree in the cemetery. He loved climbing trees.

Isabel paused for a moment and then read the verse she had asked to be inscribed on Sebastian's gravestone:

> "How precious to me are your thoughts, God!
> How vast is the sum of them!" (Psalm 139:17).

Isabel stopped reading, and I stood up and opened the square-shaped lid of the white, heavy, rectangular plastic urn that held the remains of Sebastian's earthly body. Steve, Isabel, and I each took turns scattering his ashes into the New Zealand wind. Brennan stood back and observed in silence. He understood our pain; he was there two years ago on this day when the police came to our door and told us Sebastian had died.

We all watched as the last pieces of Sebastian's former life blew across the Remarkables; the sparkles from the remnant dust specks glistened through the sun's final pink glow. We stood for a while, the three of us holding each other, Brennan next to us, staring as the sunset disappeared behind the horizon. We were all crying and yet laughing in relief. We had made it through this moment. We would be OK.

Then I recalled one of the final scenes in *The Return of the King*. Frodo never fully recovered from an injury from a Morgul-knife by a Ringwraith during the skirmish at Weathertop. On each anniversary of the stabbing, his shoulder wound would hurt again. Frodo needed to leave Middle-earth to heal from his injuries and finally find rest. Thus, he took a ship to the Grey Havens, Tolkien's version of heaven, accompanied by Gandalf, who was leaving Middle-earth as well. Merry, Pippin, and Sam began crying when they realized they were to be left behind. Gandalf's last words in Tolkien's final book of his trilogy were something to remember: "Well. Here at last, dear friends on the shore of the Sea, comes the end of our Fellowship in Middle-earth. Go in peace! I will not say: do not weep; for not all tears are an evil."[72]

And like Frodo, it was time for us to leave Middle-earth and go home.[73]

---

72 The Lord of the Rings. *Part Three: The Return of the King*. By J. R. R. Tolkien, Del Rey, 1986.

73 Baker, J. "The Mountains Melt Like Wax." *Ekstasis Magazine*, 2022, www.ekstasismagazine.com/blog/2022/the-mountains-melt-like-wax.

APPENDIX ONE

Recommended Books on Grief/Suffering

Biebel, David, and Suzanne L. Foster. *Finding Your Way After the Suicide of Someone You Love*. Zondervan Books, 2005.

Bolton, Iris, and Mitchell Curtis. *My Son...My Son...: A Guide to Healing After Death, Loss, or Suicide*. Bolton Press Atlanta, 2013.

Devine, Megan. *It's OK that You're Not OK: Meeting Grief and Loss in a Culture that Doesn't Understand. Sound Ture Inc., 2017.*

Understand. Sound True Inc., 2017.

Guthrie, Nancy. *What Grieving People Wish You Knew about What Really Helps (and What Really Hurts)*. Crossway Books, 2016.

Hearing, Merrit H. *Lessons From a Son's Life...and Death: One Man's Journey into the Mystery of Grief.* 2016.

Hodges, Samuel J., and Kathy Leonard. *Grieving with Hope.* Baker Books, 2011.

Hsu, Albert Y. *Grieving a Suicide: A Loved One's Search for Comfort, Answers, and Hope.* 2nd ed., IVP Books, 2017.

Keller, Timothy. *On Death.* Penguin Books, 2020.

Keller, Timothy. *The Songs of Jesus: A Year of Daily Devotions in the Psalms.* Viking, 2016.

Keller, Timothy. *Walking with God Through Pain and Suffering.* Penguin Books, 2016.

Lewis, C. S. *A Grief Observed.* Harper Collins Publishers, 1989.

Lewis, C. S. *The Problem of Pain.* William Collins Sons, 1978.

Ortland, Dane C. *Gentle and Lowly: The Heart of Christ for Sinners and Sufferers.* Crossway Books, 2020.

Osborn, Joy Bird, and Terry A. Osborn. *Moving Forward: A Christian Study for Survivors of Suicide Loss.* Christian Association for Survivors of Suicide Loss, Inc., 2023.

Roe, Gary. *Broken Walk: Experiencing God After the Loss of a Child.* Healing Resources Publishing, 2022.

Roe, Gary. *Shattered: Surviving the Loss of a Child.* Healing Resources Publishing, 2017.

Schulte, Rita A. *Surviving Suicide Loss: Making Your Way Beyond the Ruins.* Northfield Publishing. 2021.

Warren, Tish Harrison. *Prayer in the Night: For Those Who Work, or Watch, or Weep.* IVP Press, 2021.

Wolterstorff, Nicholas. *Lament for a Son.* William B. Eerdmans Publishing Company, 1987.

Wyman, Alexandra. *The Suicide Club: What to Do When Someone You Love Chooses Death. Houndstooth Press, 2022.*

APPENDIX TWO

Selected Psalms of Lament

Psalm 3

Psalm 4

Psalm 5

Psalm 6

Psalm 10

Psalm 13

Psalm 17

Psalm 22

Psalm 25

Psalm 30

Psalm 31

Psalm 69

Psalm 73

Psalm 77

Psalm 86

Psalm 88

Psalm 102

APPENDIX THREE

Other Selected Resources

*This is not an exhaustive list of resources; additional support options may be available.

- Suicide Hotline: 988 is the national suicide and crisis lifeline number: https://www.988lifeline.org
- Alternate Suicide Hotline Numbers: 1-800-273-TALK (1-800-273-8255) 1-800-SUICIDE (1 800-784-2433)
- Texting to a Counselor: #741741
- For Deaf, Hard of Hearing, and People with Speech Disabilities who use a TTY, call:

  1-800-799-4TTY (1-800-799-4889)
- In Washington State: https://doh.wa.gov/you-and-your-family/injury-and-violence-prevention/suicide-prevention/hotlines-text-and-chat-resources

- The National Hopeline Network: https://www.hopeline.com
- Christian Association for Survivors of Suicide Loss: https://www.suicideloss.org
- Grief Share: https://www.griefshare.org
- Alliance of Hope for Suicide Survivor: https://www.allianceofhope.org
- TAPS (Tragedy Assistance Program for Survivors: https://www.taps.org/suicidepostvention or call 1800-959-TAPS (1-800-959-8277)
- The American Association of Christian Counselors: https://www.aacc.net
- The American Association of Suicidology: https://www.suicidology.org
- The American Foundation for Suicide Prevention: https://www.afsp.org

About the Author

Jackie helps grieving mothers who have lost a child to suicide survive the seemingly unsurvivable devastation thrust upon them, guiding them not only to endure but also to thrive and grow. For the past eight years, she has walked alongside countless mothers who have lost children to suicide and other traumatic deaths, encouraging them to find beauty and hope in their brokenness by keeping their eyes fixed on Jesus and clinging to Him throughout their grief journey.

Jackie holds a doctorate in nursing practice from the University of Washington and a master's in biblical studies from Multnomah University, blending clinical expertise with compassionate faith in her work as a pediatric nurse practitioner in Vancouver, Washington. Her career has been dedicated to caring for underserved children and families, and she regularly supports families facing depression, anxiety, and suicidal thoughts with practical guidance and heartfelt prayer.

Outside of her professional life, Jackie spends her spare time quilting and traveling around the world with her husband of thirty-five years, Steve. Designing and sewing wedding gowns, elaborate costumes, and vintage clothes alongside her cats, Mr. Darcy and Jasper, is also a passion. She enjoys thrift shopping for antique books with her daughter, Isabel, and nurturing dreams of future academic pursuits in British Literature.

Jackie's journey as a writer began in childhood—her first poem, "I Have an Elf of My Own," was published at age ten in *Our Best in '73: Buffalo Public Schools*. Writing later became a vital path to healing after the loss of her son, Sebastian, to suicide. Through her Substack page and published essays in *Ekstasis Magazine* and *The Columbian* newspaper, Jackie shares stories of grief and resilience to help others discover beauty and hope amid brokenness.

She and her husband founded New Heights Clinic, a free faith-based medical clinic in Vancouver, WA, and she co-leads a grief support group at her church. She has also appeared as a guest on several podcasts, discussing topics such as grief, mental health, faith, and her personal journey, expanding her outreach and connecting with listeners who need hope the most. Passionate about helping others not only survive but thrive, Jackie is committed to finding light and hope even in life's darkest chapters.

www.ingramcontent.com/pod-product-compliance
Lightning Source LLC
LaVergne TN
LVHW091253150826
845673LV00006B/1405

* 9 7 9 8 8 9 1 8 5 4 1 2 3 *